TASTE KOREA

Korean recipes with local ingredients

Ae Jin Huys

Lannoo

CONTENTS

One of the earliest memories from my short-lived childhood in Korea is that of the earthen jars (*onggi*) in our garden. They contained homemade *jang* and I still remember often sneaking by and stealthily dipping my finger in them. And though I rediscovered this taste only many years later, I am convinced that these Korean umami flavours have strongly influenced my taste buds all this time.

With this recipe book, I want to share with others the wonder that carries me on my quest to rediscover Korean cuisine. And where else to start than with its essence, the well-known *jang* that so typifies Korean cooking. *Jang* always refers to the three most important seasonings: fermented soy sauce, soybean paste, and chilli paste (*gangjang, doenjang, gochujang*).

Over the years I have collected countless Korean recipes by tasting in numerous eateries, watching housewives at the stove, receiving teaching from many chefs and, of course, scouring the omniscient digital information network. Yet over time, progressively, I learned to develop my own personal taste and to adapt classical Korean recipes by cooking with local ingredients.

This is how the concept of my second cookbook was created: if you have one or more jars of jang at home, you can open this book on any humdrum evening and cook Korean. For a more festive meal, you can select specific recipes for sharing dishes and serve them Korean style. On top of that, you will find recipes from my masters – including how to make jang yourself, a challenge for the more experienced fermentation enthusiasts. Here I hope to pass along some of their inspiring vision and their stories, offering a view of food that differs from a mere routine pleasure or daily obligation.

먹자!

MOKJA! LET'S EAT!

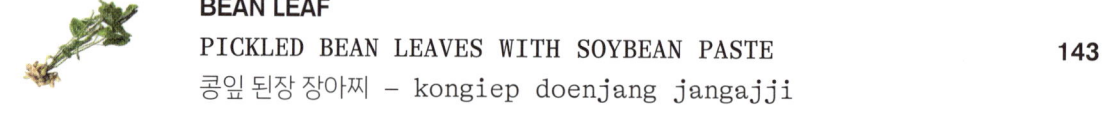
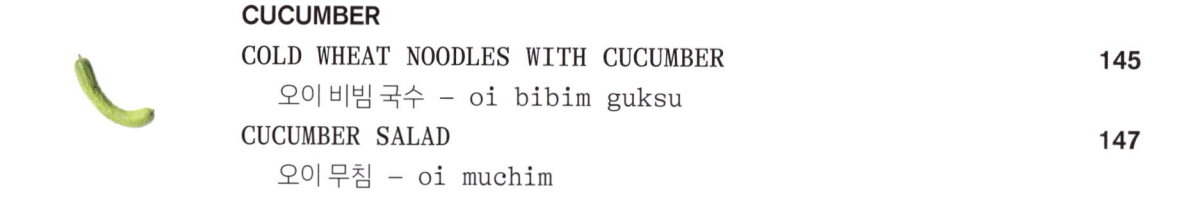

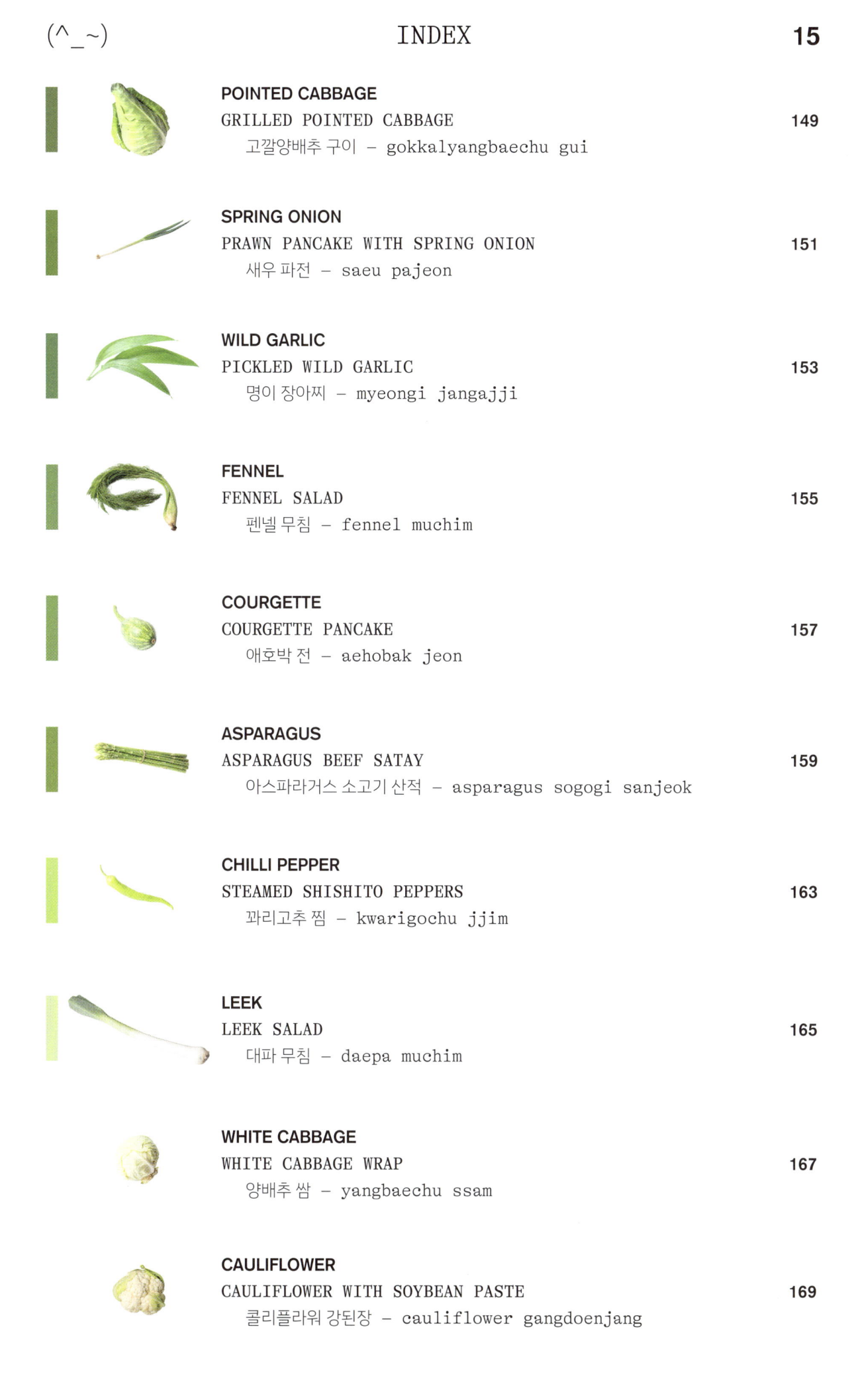

The words *yang-nyeom*, meaning 'seasoning' in Korean, originated from two words: *yak*, which means medicine, and *nyeom*, which means thinking or thought. As its etymology indicates, *yang-nyeom* was once used as a medicine, and today it is used to improve the flavour of food. A cook must fully put heart and mind into the food preparation, using fresh seasonal ingredients and *yang-nyeom* to create a dish that is more than a meal, but also a natural medicine for body and soul.
"One must reflect on which ingredients are used, where they are from, how they are prepared and by whom, and how they will affect the body. Eating according to what the body needs, rather than what the palate desires, is essential."

– Wook Wan Seunim

The Buddhist monk Wook Wan has been certified as 'Master of Korean Temple Food' by the Jogye Order, the largest Buddhist order in Korea. She has dedicated her life to the temple cuisine and its associated philosophy at home and abroad. Wook Wan published the first English language cookbook on Korean temple cuisine, entitled *Wookwan's Korean Temple Food: The Road to the Taste of Enlightenment*, which received an award in the cookbook category at the annual Benjamin Franklin Awards in 2019.

KOREAN TEMPLE CUISINE, A VISIONARY VIEW OF NUTRITION

Until the 14th century, Buddhism was one of the most important religions in Korea, with a strong influence on society, culture, and philosophy and, by extension, on Korean food culture and philosophy.

For Korean Buddhists, nutrition is an essential part of religious life. Accordingly, the basic philosophy refers to the conscious and enlightened handling of food. Concerned with promoting harmony and health in nature and in people, Buddhist temple food contains no animal products. In addition, the use of the five strongly flavoured, energising ingredients (onion, garlic, chives, spring onion and leek) is restricted in order to maintain a calm, meditative state of mind. Food is prepared with a profound understanding of local ingredients and their natural aromas. This cuisine is based on an in-depth knowledge, collected over centuries, of local ingredients, like wild roots, stems, leaves, nuts, fruit, and flowers from the area. With these, a natural, plant-based and seasonal diet was developed, offering a traditional Korean answer to the western interest in vegan food.

양념장
YANGNYEOMJANG

seasoning

Yangnyeomjang refers to the seasoning that adds taste to a dish. The essence of *yangnyeomjang* is to accentuate the original flavour and to prolong the shelf life of your basic ingredients. The selection of seasonings in the appropriate proportions defines the dish and reveals something of the chef's style.

손맛
SONMAT

hand taste

Sonmat can be literally translated as 'hand taste' and refers to the ability to flavour a dish 'by feel', to select the optimal combination and quantity of *yangnyeomjang* by hand.

Korean chefs and homemakers often speak of 'an appropriate amount' instead of exact weights and measures. *Sonmat* is about much more than a perfectly executed dish. It refers to the power that a particular dish or cooking style can have to evoke the memories of everything it elicits. *Sonmat* also conveys the chef's personality, the setting and the experience of eating, the nostalgia and emotion evoked when smelling or tasting a dish, or the simple experience of just thinking about it. *Sonmat* is often mentioned in the same breath as mother, recollections of the savoury delights of childhood, and the love we can feel while eating a meal.

Scientifically, it is no less fascinating to consider the microflora of the hands, which are, ultimately, one of the basic ingredients of every preparation.

시원한맛
SIWEONHANMAT

sixth sense

Siweonhanmat is the extra dimension beyond taste and smell, specifically the sensation the body experiences as an essential element of a meal. In our modern civilisation, the experience of smell and taste has taken on a prominent place, but the importance of food in promoting a healthy digestion was already part of traditional Korean food culture from the beginning of the 16th century. Scientific research has now established links between a healthy intestinal flora and mental health. Intestinal cells are said to play an important part in producing serotonin, also referred to as the 'happiness hormone'.

발효
BALHYO

fermentation

Jang (fermented seasonings) is often referred to as the essence of Korean cuisine, but *kimchi* (fermented vegetables) has captured worldwide attention thanks to the beneficial probiotics present in *kimchi*. Generally, fermentation (*balhyo*) plays a central role in Korean cuisine.

Many cultures use fermentation as a technique for preserving food. It is a natural process to transform certain nutrients using bacteria, fungi, and yeasts. A successful fermentation process leads to a change in the taste, smell, and texture of a product, making it more digestible and healthier for the body. The Korean fermentation method is based on the knowledge and application of micro-organisms occurring naturally in ingredients and in the environment.

슬로푸드
SLOW FOOD

slow food

There are no original Korean words for 'slow food' but, as my friend and mentor Go Young Joo (a Korean chocolatier who runs Cacaoboom) aptly puts it: "Korean food was simply slow food itself." Fermented products, such as *jang* and *kimchi*, are in effect another way of cooking food slowly. According to the ancient Korean philosophy of eating, fermentation is associated with the aesthetics of waiting. Slowly fermented foods have a rich taste with subtle differences and, depending on the region, the season, and the chef, these nuances appear endless.

장
JANG

fermented seasonings

Jang refers to fermented sauce made from soybeans, water, and salt. Salt has a prominent place in many world cuisines, and Korea developed a salty flavour in fermented sauces containing amino acids, derived from beans with salt added. Traditionally, *jang* was prepared in the autumn and winter after harvesting the soybeans. It is intensive work that takes weeks or even months and is often viewed as the most important task in a household. Typically, a household was known for the quality of its *jang*. Countless traditional sayings show how strongly *jang* is intertwined with the history and food culture of Koreans. Some examples:

장이 단집에 복이 많다.
Fortunate is the house with tasty *jang*.

주인집 장 떨어지자, 나그네 장 마단다.
When the host's *jang* runs out, the traveller will decline the soup.

장이 달아야 국이 달다.
The soup is savoury where the *jang* is good.

장은 묵은 장맛이 좋다.
Old *jang* tastes better.

콩
KONG

soybean

Since grain was the main staple in the Korean diet, there was often a shortage of proteins and fats. Soybeans (kong) were a welcome addition and were called 'the meat of the field', thanks to their high percentage of proteins and fats. Along with rice, barley and millet, soybeans became one of the most widely consumed agricultural crops. They have many applications in Korean cuisine. In their natural form, they are pressed into oil or germinated to produce soy shoots. The leaves of the plant are pickled or served as lettuce. Ground and boiled, soybeans provide the basis of soy milk and tofu. Roasted and ground into powder, you can mix them into drinks and rice cakes.

By fermenting soybeans, complex seasonings were created with a deep umami flavour, and the fermentation process itself provided an optimal way to make soy proteins more digestible.

소금
SOGEUM

salt

Salt (*sogeum*) is one of the three basic ingredients for making soy sauce and soybean paste. The salt used for this purpose is purified sea salt. Since sea salt contains harmful substances present in sea water (alongside sodium and minerals), it is healthier when purified. One method to remove these substances is by heating, washing, rinsing, and drying. Some experts swear by salt that has been dried for up to three years, or an even more exclusive form: Korean bamboo salt, which is cooked up to nine times in bamboo tubes at high temperature until it turns purple. In bygone days, bamboo salt was administered as a medicine for its healing properties. Purified salt is an essential ingredient for *jang* and is also used to prevent spoiling.

메주, 간장, 된장

MEJU, GANJANG, DOENJANG

fermented soybeans, soy sauce, soybean
paste

Soy sauce (*ganjang*) and soybean paste (*doenjang*) are the product of a single production process that consists of three fermentation procedures. Soybeans are washed, soaked, and boiled. The boiled beans are crushed, shaped, and then dried to make the *meju*. To initiate a natural fermentation process, rice stalks are added, cultivating the natural micro-organisms that are essential to the *meju*. The *meju* is then placed in large earthenware jars, and water with a saline solution of at least 20% is added for a second fermentation cycle that takes several months. In spring, the liquid is decanted for soy sauce and the solid soybean bricks are pureed to make soybean paste. Finally, the young soy sauce and soybean paste are allowed to mature separately for long periods of time. A traditionally produced soy sauce is usually matured for at least one year.

In modern Korea, you will find all kinds of *jang*, from cheap commercial products to exclusive, vintage artisanal varieties. Broadly, you can divide the various *ganjang* into traditional soy sauce and commercial soy sauce. *Hansik ganjang*, *joseon ganjang* and *jip ganjang* are some of the names for traditional Korean soy sauce, prepared according to traditional methods and containing only the basic ingredients (soybeans, salt, water). Yet the most common name for this type is *guk ganjang*, literally 'soup soy sauce', which refers to how it is used today. *Guk ganjang* is generally a salty soy sauce that should be added carefully as a seasoning. This generic soy sauce is further divided into different subtypes according to the fermentation length:

- ○ 햇간장, *haet ganjang* is soy sauce that has fermented for about one year.
- ○ 중간장, *jung ganjang* refers to fermented soy sauce that is several years old.
- ○ 진간장, *jin ganjang* has fermented for at least five years.

Soy sauce that is produced commercially and on a large scale has a very short fermentation time due to the incorporation of various additives. Two variants in this category can be found worldwide. In what can only be described as a misleading marketing ploy, one of these soy sauces was dubbed *jin ganjang*, despite it being far removed from the original *jin ganjang*. A second variant is the soy sauce that is most frequently found in western households and that resembles the commercial Japanese variant: *yangjo ganjang*, which is brewed in a similar way and has a sweeter taste due to the addition of wheat.

청국장
CHEONGGUKJANG

`fast fermented soybean paste`

A traditional seasoning that occupies a less prominent place among the other *jang* is *cheonggukjang*, a rapidly fermented soybean paste. It is a simplified but very healthy soybean paste, which can be consumed after only a few days. Soybeans are washed, soaked, boiled or steamed, and then fermented at high temperature for two to three days. The fermentation process produces a scum and a strong smell that other *jang* do not have. Therefore, this paste is not easily appreciated by everyone. Before use, *cheonggukjang* is often seasoned with chilli powder and salt and mashed into a paste. You can only keep this paste fresh for a few days (somewhat longer in the freezer).

고추장
GOCHUJANG

`chilli paste`

The arrival of chilli peppers in the 17th century heralded the beginning of all sorts of spicy Korean dishes. The best-known contemporary kimchi varieties have chilli peppers as an ingredient. Chilli also became an important seasoning for *jang*. For instance, chilli paste (*gochujang*) is one of the three most important seasonings in modern Korean cuisine. A basic recipe usually includes dried red chilli powder (*gochugaru*), ground fermented soybeans (*mejugaru*), fermented rice syrup (*ssaljocheong*), rice flour (*chapssalgaru*), and salt (*sogeum*). But practically every maker will have their own version. For example, during my last trip to Korea, I learned to make chilli paste with strawberries (*dalgi gochujang*) from *jang* master Yun Wang Soon (see p. 52).
Ideally, chilli paste must ferment for at least six months in a sunny place before use.

고추가루
GOCHUGARU

`chilli powder`

In a Korean market you will typically find about 3000 types of chilli pepper. Their flavours are largely determined by the conditions in which the chillies are grown: the climate, the soil, and the cultivation method. Producers usually select one or more varieties to compose their *gochugaru*. Even with a balanced blend of non-spicy, medium to very spicy varieties, it is difficult to determine which ones were used. Most Koreans prefer *taeyangcho* chilli powder, produced from peppers that were dried in the sun, turning their stems yellow and their flesh red. You can discover different kinds of chilli powder depending on the region: chilli in northern areas is ground more coarsely, while certain chilli powders from the south still have seeds.

쌀조청
SSALJOCHEONG

`rice syrup`

Ssaljocheong, or rice syrup, is used to sweeten dishes. It is also one of the ingredients for *gochujang*. Rice syrup is produced by fermenting boiled rice and sprouted wheat together at low temperature. The enzymes from the sprouted wheat convert the starch from the rice into sugars. This sweet liquid is then boiled until most of the moisture has evaporated and a thick syrup has formed. The malty taste of the rice syrup stems from the fermentation process itself.

찹쌀
CHAPSSAL

glutinous rice

Chapssal, or glutinous rice, is different from *maepssal*, the type of rice typically served at the table. *Chapssal* and *chapssalgaru* (glutinous rice flour) are both processed into distinct types of *jang*. When glutinous rice flour is not available, flour from wheat, barley, and millet are acceptable substitutes.

장독
JANGDOK

earthen jar

Jangdok are large earthenware jars for storing fermented foods. Food storage in ceramic pots is said to date back to prehistoric times in Korea. These pots were found wherever Koreans lived, regardless of region or class. Pottery was cheap and the microporous structure of the material made it especially suitable for fermentation. Over time, the golden age of potters became superseded by industrialization, and today only a handful of Korean potters are masters of the original craft. 옹 *ong* means 'pottery'; earthenware pots are also called 옹기 *onggi*. Smaller jars are 항아리 *hangari* and 단지 *danji*.

장독대
JANGDOKDAE

terrace for jangdok

The word *jangdokdae* is derived from *jangdok* which means 'jar', while *dae* denotes 'a place'. *Jangdok* are generally grouped together and stored outside on a terrace of some sort, *jangdokdae*. Today, *jangdok* can still be seen alongside most houses in the Korean countryside. 옹기종기 *Onggi jongi* is the term for a warm sense of togetherness and refers to the various *onggi* standing together.

○   Except for recipes by Korean chefs, manufacturers and cultural translator Chung Chung Kee, all recipes are for one serving.

○   Fermented pastes such as *doenjang* (soybean paste) and *gochujang* (chilli paste) are usually found in Asian supermarkets and stores or retailers with a more adventurous offer. They are typically sold in plastic boxes, available in various sizes and volumes.

○   Most Korean soy sauces outside of Korea are commercially produced, and their taste is comparable to the Japanese variant, which can be substituted (see p. 23). If you come across Korean soy sauce, this will most likely be the commercial *jin ganjan*. Since this book has been created for a Western audience, the recipes have been prepared with this latter variety of soy sauce.

○   Ingredients such as toasted sesame oil, seaweeds such as kelp and *miyeok* (*wakame* in Japanese), tofu and rice syrup can be normally found at your local bio shop.

Is something missing?
Feel free to contact me for any questions you might have.

듬
장
아
찌

PICKLED VEGETABLES WITH SOY SAUCE*

INGREDIENTS

central part of 1
Chinese cabbage (sweeter
and more tender)
¼ daikon
¼ kohlrabi
100g mushrooms

BRINE WATER

400ml soy sauce
400ml brown rice vinegar
400g muscovado sugar

PREPARATION

Rinse the vegetables and chop into large chunks. Put them in a 3-litre mason jar. Bring the brine to the boil in a pot. Take the pot off the heat as soon as the liquid boils and pour over the vegetables. Make sure the vegetables stay immersed in the brine. Leave overnight. Take the vegetables from the mason jar and cook them again. Allow the boiled brine to cool. Put the vegetables back in the jar, pour over the brine, and allow to mature in the refrigerator. After two weeks, the flavours will have matured well, and after three months (or more), this dish will still be delicious.

GOOD TO KNOW

For convenience, I added lots of vegetables. To get started, you can use any kind or quantity of vegetables you have to hand at home. The brine can be boiled again to be reused a few more times.

*   RECIPE BY MOON SUN HEE.

Korea's Moon Sung Hee is a well-known 'natural food researcher'. She cooks, studies, teaches, and writes about natural vegan nutrition. Driven by a deep belief in people, nature, and how food has the power to harmonise, Moon Sung Hee has been involved in various social projects focused on food. She has published several cookbooks, and runs her own cooking studio, Peaceful Table, together with her daughter Sol.

For me, 'nature' is everything that is connected to life. It bothers me when the word 'environment' is used instead of 'nature'. It sounds misleading, as if we humans are at the centre, and nature is our environment. When you eat an orange, you are also eating the sunlight, the water, earth and wind that fed the orange tree. Then, you become the sunlight, the water, the earth, and the wind. I think that is nature... This is why you are what you eat.

– Moon Sung Hee

STEW OF PICKLED VEGETABLES WITH SOY SAUCE*

INGREDIENTS

½ pickled Chinese
cabbage (see p. 31)
1 to 2 tablespoons
fermented soybean paste
3 tablespoons perilla
oil (see p. 119) or rice
bran oil
400ml vegetable stock
(from daikon, onion,
spring onion, kelp)
1 Spanish green chilli
pepper

PREPARATION

Gently squeeze the liquid out of the cabbage.
Place all the ingredients in a cooking pot and
allow to cook with the lid on. Chop the chilli
finely and add at the end to steam.

---

*   RECIPE BY MOON SUN HEE.

밀피유나베

HOTPOT OF CHINESE CABBAGE AND BEEF STEAKS

INGREDIENTS

150g beef steaks, 0.5cm thick
1 Chinese cabbage
a bunch of perilla (see p. 119)
5g kelp
200ml water

MARINADE

1 garlic clove, minced
2 tablespoons soy sauce
2 tablespoons rice syrup (see p. 24)
pinch of black pepper
1 teaspoon toasted sesame oil

DIPPING SAUCE

2 tablespoons soy sauce
1 tablespoon rice wine or water
1 teaspoon rice syrup (see p. 24)
1 teaspoon vinegar

PREPARATION

Combine all the marinade ingredients and mix well. Add the steaks and let them marinate in the refrigerator for at least half an hour. Remove the bottom core of the cabbage and peel off the leaves. Rinse and drain. On a cutting board, make layers starting with a leaf of Chinese cabbage followed by a slice of marinated beef and two to three leaves of perilla on top. Repeat this pattern and cover the top layer with an additional cabbage leaf. Cut the layers into even 5cm pieces. Take a casserole dish or Korean ttukbaegi or, alternatively, a small saucepan with a 10-12cm diameter. Place the kelp on the bottom of this pot and put the previously prepared millefeuille pieces on top. Start at the outer edges and move towards the centre, arranging them vertically so that you can see the various layers. Add the water, keeping it at least 1.5 centimetres below the rim. Bring to the boil on medium heat. Cover with a lid and simmer for another 15 minutes or until all the ingredients are cooked. Serve the hotpot while still warm. Dip each bite (package of three flavours) in the dipping sauce and savour the taste.

GOOD TO KNOW

Millefeuille refers to the famous French puff pastry dessert with 'thousands of layers'.
Nabe is a popular Japanese hotpot dish. The Korean version is delicious with marinated beef and perilla, which gives it a specific flavour. If you don't have perilla, *shiso* is an alternative, but you can also do without. For a more festive dish, you can fill the centre of the hotpot with mushrooms (enoki, shiitake, oyster mushroom) and then heat it up.
A ttukbaegi is an earthenware pot, widely used in Korean cuisine, that is placed on the stove. Typically, a *ttukbaegi* is brought to the table where it keeps your meal warm.

Koh Eun Jeong was my first 'teacher,' and she has been a guide to many other Korean homemakers and renowned chefs alike. Her craft is admirable. She used to be a teacher and that shines through. She excels at translating her wonderful *sonmat* (see p. 20) into recipes with just the right quantities and proportions. All the dishes from her hand that I tasted are simple, pure, wholesome, and packed with flavour. With a profound knowledge of authentic Korean cuisine, she has dubbed herself 'a food culture activist'. The following recipe was transmitted to me by her. I invented a more local variant using cauliflower (see recipe on p. 169).

팽이버섯강된장

ENOKI AND SOYBEAN PASTE SEASONING*

INGREDIENTS

½ onion
½ thin leek
1 pack of enoki
3 tablespoons soybean
paste
2 cloves of garlic,
minced
½ Spanish green chilli
pepper, finely chopped
100ml water

PREPARATION

Chop the onion and finely shred the leek. Remove
the enoki feet and cut the remainder into equal
0.5cm pieces. Put water in a pot and dissolve the
soybean paste. Add the chopped vegetables, garlic,
and chilli pepper and bring everything to the
boil. Simmer until it is cooked and the flavours
have nicely melded. Serve as a savoury seasoning
with a bowl of rice (see p. 41).

*   RECIPE BY KOH EUN JEONG.

RICE WITH DAIKON

INGREDIENTS

¼ daikon (150g)
1 teaspoon toasted
sesame oil
150g cooked rice*

SAUS

1 garlic clove, minced
1 tablespoon soy sauce
1 tablespoon toasted
sesame oil
1 tablespoon toasted
sesame seeds
½ spring onion, finely
chopped
1 teaspoon chilli powder
(optional)

PREPARATION

Peel the daikon and julienne it into thin 8cm
strips. Cook the daikon al dente and drain. Mix
with the sesame oil. Arrange the boiled rice in
a bowl and top with daikon. Make the sauce by
mixing all the ingredients and serve alongside as
a seasoning.

GOOD TO KNOW

*   Basic recipe for rice

Rinse the rice until the water turns clear, then add fresh water in a ratio
of 1:1. Soak for 30 minutes, cook gently under closed lid for 20 minutes.
Wait another 10 minutes before removing the lid and stir to loosen it up.

Here is an alternative when you have a rice cooker at home: rinse 2 cups of
rice until the water turns clear. Put the rice in the rice cooker and top
up with the right amount of water. Place the julienne sliced daikon on top.
Cook the rice as normal and serve the mubap with the sauce.

마 늘 장 아 찌

PICKLED GARLIC

INGREDIENTS

8-10 bulbs of garlic

BRINE WATER

100ml soy sauce
250ml water
150ml natural vinegar
100g cane sugar
5g kelp (optional)
2 dried shiitakes
(optional)

PREPARATION

Immerse the unpeeled garlic cloves in a bowl of water. Soak for at least 3 hours. The cloves will now be easy to peel. Remove the ends if necessary and place the garlic in a glass mason jar. Meanwhile, make the brine by mixing all other ingredients and heat up until boiling point. Pour the hot brine over the garlic. Make sure that the cloves remain submerged (if necessary, put a weight on) and close the mason jar. Allow to cool at room temperature. Repeat the next day: pour off into a pan the brine water and bring it to a boil for a second time. Pour it once again over the garlic in the mason jar and let cool before storing in the refrigerator.

GOOD TO KNOW

This recipe is easier to execute with fresh garlic. Unlike dried garlic, fresh garlic does not need to be peeled and can be pickled whole. Just rinse the bulbs before and cut off the stems.

마약계란장

DRUG EGGS WITH SOY SAUCE

INGREDIENTS

1 tablespoon vinegar
pinch of salt
3 eggs
water, to boil the eggs
ice cubes (optional)
1 tablespoon toasted
sesame oil
2 tablespoons toasted
sesame seeds

BRINE WATER

50ml soy sauce
100ml water
2 tablespoons rice syrup
(see p. 24)
1 tablespoon rice
vinegar
3 wafer-thin ginger
slices
1 garlic clove, bruised
1 spring onion, finely
chopped
½ or 1 Spanish red
chilli pepper, finely
chopped
½ or 1 Spanish green
chilli pepper, finely
chopped

PREPARATION

Prepare the brine by mixing all the ingredients. Bring the water to the boil, add vinegar and salt, and cook the eggs for 6 minutes. Spoon the eggs into a bowl of ice-cold water to cool. Peel the eggs – the easiest way to do this is by keeping them under water. Place them directly in the brine. Marinate for a minimum of 3 hours and a maximum of 6 hours (the longer you marinate the eggs, the saltier they become). Serve with a bowl of rice (see p. 41), dressed with a tablespoon of brine for added flavour.

GOOD TO KNOW

The remaining brine can be kept in the refrigerator for some time. It is delicious cold as a broth with boiled wheat noodles or as a seasoning for finely chopped cucumber salad. It can also serve as a base for marinades or dips.
'마약계란' literally translates to 'drug eggs'. According to Korean friends, the name was once invented by a market vendor in Gwangjang Sijang, one of the oldest and largest traditional markets in South Korea. As a kind of sales gimmick, she developed *mayak gimbap*, a smaller version of *gimbap*, the popular seaweed rice rolls. Since then, several other dishes have been developed with the name *mayak*, such as *mayak gyeran*. *Mayak* means 'drugs' and refers to the captivating taste that is bound to make you long for more.

닭도리탕

SPICY CHICKEN STEW

INGREDIENTS

400g chicken thighs
500ml water
2 to 3 potatoes (200 g)
½ carrot (optional)
1 onion
¼ leek

SAUCE

2 tablespoons chilli
paste
2 to 3 cloves of garlic,
crushed
2 tablespoons rice syrup
(see p. 24)
4 tablespoons soy sauce
1 slice of ginger
1 Spanish red chilli
pepper (optional)

PREPARATION

Blanch the chicken thighs in boiling water until
the meat turns opaque. Rinse with cold water
and drain. Peel the potatoes and onion and
scrape the carrot clean. Cut the vegetables into
pieces of roughly equal size. Thoroughly mix all
the ingredients for the sauce together. Bring
everything (except the leek) to the boil on medium
heat. Once the water boils, lower the heat and put
on the lid. Check and stir at regular intervals.
Skim off the surface fat and check frequently if
the meat is cooked by inserting a skewer. Slice
the leek into small rounds and add to the dish
just before serving.

BRAISED CHICKEN

INGREDIENTS

1 farm chicken (1.3kg)
3 potatoes
2 carrots
1 onion

AROMATICS

8 tablespoons soy sauce
8 tablespoons rice syrup
(see p. 24)
8 large cloves of
garlic, crushed
8 black peppercorns
1 spring onion
1 Spanish red chilli
pepper
pinch of chilli powder
(optional)

PREPARATION

Blanch the chicken in boiling water until the meat turns opaque. Rinse thoroughly with cold water. Bring the chicken to a second boil in fresh water with the aromatics added. Cook for an hour on medium heat, turning the chicken regularly to cook evenly. At frequent intervals, remove the scum from the surface until the liquid is clear. Peel and cut the vegetables into coarse, equal-sized pieces. Add these to the chicken and simmer gently until everything is cooked.

GOOD TO KNOW

You can also chop the chicken into pieces before cooking (thigh and breast) or order a jointed chicken from the butcher. Make sure that the skin is left on since this gives the dish its rich aroma. If the chicken has been jointed, the vegetables can be added earlier. You can add some extra chilli powder for a spicier version.

이북식 닭무침

NORTH-KOREAN CHICKEN SALAD*

INGREDIENTS

1 farm chicken
1 to 2 litres of water
1 cucumber

AROMATICS

1 bulb of garlic
1 bunch of spring onions
10 black peppercorns

SAUCE

1 spring onion
3 cloves of garlic,
minced
1 tablespoon soy sauce
2 to 3 tablespoons
chilli powder
1 tablespoon yellow
mustard
pinch of ground pepper
1 tablespoon toasted
sesame oil

PREPARATION

Bring a whole farm chicken to the boil in the water with the aromatics. Remove the scum with a skimmer and repeat until all of the scum has gone. Place the cooked chicken on a dish. When cool, remove the skin and tear the chicken into bite-sized pieces. Halve the cucumber lengthwise and cut into diagonal 0.5cm slices. Brine with a pinch of salt, and after 10 minutes remove the released moisture. Mix the chicken and cucumber with the ingredients for the sauce.

*   RECIPE BY YUN WANG SOON.

South Korea has a 'food master' policy that promotes recognition and support for master experts in producing, processing, and preparing top-notch traditional Korean food. Over 80 master experts have already received recognition for various traditional products and preparations, with only a few of them in the *jang* category, the traditional Korean fermented sauces. One such expert is Yun Wang Soon, recognized as Korean food master No. 50.

Yun Wang Soon was born in Gyeongcheon-myeon, Wanju-gun, Jeollabuk-do, the fifth child in a family of three boys and seven girls. She was the third daughter and they said she was a gifted cook.

By planting and growing soybeans with my mother and making them into soy sauce, soybean paste, and chilli paste, I learned to appreciate and create the traditional Korean *jang* taste a bit better each time. My mother was worried that her daughter had taken on too burdensome a task. Then she died and left me with the responsibility to preserve and further develop her *jang* flavour, which remains so dear to me.

I have also been fortunate enough to learn a lot about traditional nutrition methods from my master, Professor Yoon Sookja. Thanks to her, my heartfelt wish to continue my mother's legacy is now being fulfilled. With the *sonmat* (see p. 20) that I inherited from her and with Yoon Sookja's knowledge of traditional dishes, I work hard until the day when I am the only expert, recognized by many, mastering an art that can be imitated by no one. I will undoubtedly become a grandmaster who can look back proudly at her two teachers.

– Yun Wang Soon

"To know the taste in that house, just have a look at their *jangdok* (see p. 27). If it is clean and orderly, the taste of their *jang* will also be good." "A tasty *jang* makes a tasty meal." And: "Pickles that you can eat all year round are a real treat." My mother entrusted me with these valuable lessons as if she foresaw the future — her third daughter's calling to pass on all *jang* knowledge to the world. After a past of poverty where food was very precious, she preserved these flavours for her family with carefully prepared *jang*.

– Yun Wang Soon

농어 회 무침

SEA BASS SALAD

INGREDIENTS

½ carrot
¼ red onion
⅓ thin cucumber
150g sea bass fillet,
skinned
½ spring onion

SAUCE

1 tablespoon chilli
paste
1 tablespoon apple cider
vinegar
1 tablespoon rice syrup
(see p. 24)
1 garlic clove, minced
1 teaspoon toasted
sesame seeds

PREPARATION

Finely slice the carrot, red onion, and cucumber into 2mm slices. Slice the sea bass similarly. Chop the spring onion diagonally into 4cm pieces. Make the sauce by mixing the ingredients. Add the sauce to the fish and vegetables and let the dish sit for a while. Serve as a fresh salad or with rice (see p. 41).

오징어 볶음

FRIED SQUID

INGREDIENTS

250g squid tubes,
cleaned
½ onion
½ Spanish red chilli
pepper, finely chopped
1 tablespoon vegetable
oil, to fry
pinch of salt

SAUCE

1 to 2 tablespoons
chilli paste
1 tablespoon soy sauce
1 tablespoon water
1 tablespoon rice syrup
(see p. 24)
2 cloves of garlic,
minced
1 teaspoon grated ginger
1 tablespoon toasted
sesame oil

PREPARATION

Rinse the squid under running water. Remove any
cartilage. Cut open the tubes and, with a sharp
knife, carve parallel lines at 0.5cm intervals.
Rotate the tube one-quarter turn and again carve
parallel lines. Now cut the tubes into 2cm strips.
Slice the onion into half rings to a thickness
of 0.3cm. Heat the oil in a pan and stir fry the
onion and chilli with the squid for 30 seconds.
Remove the pan from the heat. Make the marinade by
mixing all the ingredients. Add the marinade to
the pan and stir fry together for a few seconds
until the squid has turned tender.

GRILLED PORK SATAY

돼
지
맥
적
구
이

INGREDIENTS

200g pork steaks, 0.5cm
thick

MARINADE

1 tablespoon soybean
paste
1 teaspoon soy sauce
2 tablespoons water
2 tablespoons rice syrup
(see p. 24)
1 garlic clove, minced
pinch of ground black
pepper

PREPARATION

Make the marinade by mixing the ingredients.
Marinate the steaks for at least one hour. Skewer
the meat on satay sticks and grill them on the
barbecue, in the grill pan or oven without adding
extra fat. Allow the edges to caramelize nicely.

족
발

BRAISED PORK SHANK

INGREDIENTS

1 pork shank with bone
(1.5kg)
1.5 litres of water

AROMATICS

1 spring onion
1 onion
1 apple, peeled
5 cloves of garlic,
crushed
5 peppercorns
2 slices of ginger
2 cloves
1 bay leaf
½ star anise
½ stick of cinnamon
2 tablespoons soybean
paste
6 tablespoons soy sauce
4 tablespoons rice wine
or soju
2 tablespoons rice syrup
(see p. 24)
1 tablespoon brown sugar

PREPARATION

Place the shank in a pot and immerse it in water.
Put a lid on the pot and let the shank soak for at
least 4 hours. Rinse the shank under cold running
water. Blanch it in boiling water until the meat
turns opaque. Rinse again under running water to
remove any cloudy liquid. Clean the pot, put it
back on the heat and bring the shank to a boil
with 1.5 litres of water and the aromatics. When
it comes to the boil, lower the heat and cover the
pot with a lid. Simmer for 1 to 1.5 hours or until
the meat is cooked. Remove the shank from the
broth and let it cool. When the meat has turned
tender, shred it into thin strips using forks, as
with 'pulled pork'.

GOOD TO KNOW

Jokbal is a popular street dish often found in traditional Korean markets.
It is delicious in a sandwich or tortilla but could just as well be served
with a tasty potato mash.

근대잡채

GLASS NOODLES WITH CHARD

INGREDIENTS

120g glass noodles
(*dangmyeon*)
½ bunch of chard (150g)
vegetable oil, to fry
pinch of sugar
1 teaspoon toasted
sesame seeds

SAUCE

2 tablespoons soy sauce
1 garlic clove, minced
1 tablespoon water
1 teaspoon sugar
1 tablespoon perilla oil
(see p. 119)
pinch of ground black
pepper

PREPARATION

Soak the glass noodles in water for half an
hour. Meanwhile, rinse and drain the chard. Pull
the leaves from the stalks and tear into bite-
sized pieces, keeping them separate. Julienne the
stalks. Stir fry the stalks in vegetable oil, stir
fry the leaves separately. Always add a pinch of
sugar to dampen the chard's slight bitterness.
Boil the noodles al dente using the water they
were soaked in. Drain the noodles in a colander
and rinse thoroughly in cold running water until
cooled to room temperature. Shake the sieve, and
let the noodles drain. Make the sauce by mixing
the ingredients, and then heat it in a wok. Add
the noodles and season with a pinch of salt and
pepper. Mix in the chard and serve with toasted
sesame seeds.

GOOD TO KNOW

Dangmyeon are Korean glass noodles, made from sweet potato starch.
You can easily substitute the chard with other leafy greens (cabbage,
spinach, purslane, etc.), but also with mushrooms, carrot, carrot greens,
and marinated beef, for instance. *Japchae* with rice is known as *japchaebap*,
another delicious dish.

문어 펜 넬 무 침

FENNEL SALAD WITH OCTOPUS

INGREDIENTS

150g octopus
coarse salt for
scrubbing the octopus
fennel salad
(see recipe p. 155)

PREPARATION

Scrub the octopus with the coarse salt, then rinse thoroughly. Cook the octopus in boiling water for 8 to 10 minutes and rinse immediately with cold water. Drain. Cut the thick tentacles into thin 0.5cm discs. Chop the fine octopus parts into bite-sized pieces. Serve with fennel salad as a side dish or mix it into a large salad.

BEEF TARTARE

INGREDIENTS

100g beef knuckle (pelé royal or mouse steak)
1 teaspoon toasted sesame oil
1 spring onion
10 grilled pine nuts

SAUCE

¼ pear
1 garlic clove
1 tablespoon soy sauce
pinch of ground black pepper

PREPARATION

Soak the steak in cold water for half an hour. Rinse with fresh cold water and pat dry with paper towels. Cut the meat into very small pieces and mix with the toasted sesame oil. Keep the meat separate in a bowl in the freezer, or on a dish with ice cubes. Meanwhile, finely chop the spring onion. Chop the pine nuts finely. Puree the pear, garlic, soy sauce and pepper until smooth. Now combine everything together. If you double the recipe, you can add a raw egg yolk for an extra creamy beef tartare.

BRAISED BEEF RIB

갈
비
찜

INGREDIENTS

300g beef rib
½ carrot
½ onion
2 shiitakes
5 chestnuts

MARINADE

2 tablespoons soy sauce
2 tablespoons water
1 tablespoon rice syrup
(see p. 24)
10 tablespoons water
2 cloves of garlic,
minced
½cm ginger
¼ pear
pinch of ground pepper
pinch of salt

PREPARATION

Soak the meat in water for fifteen minutes to remove the blood. Rinse, pat dry, and blanch for 5 minutes. Rinse. Finely chop the ingredients for the marinade and mix well with the liquid ingredients, salt, and pepper. Marinate the meat for 1.5 hours. Meanwhile, clean the vegetables and cut them into coarse, equally sized pieces of 2cm thick. Stew the meat at medium temperature in a pot. After 10 minutes, set the heat to a low temperature and mix in the vegetables. Let it simmer under a closed lid until everything is cooked.

소
고
기
불
고
기

MARINATED BEEF SLICES

INGREDIENTS

200g ribeye steak*
¼ onion
1 spring onion
vegetable oil, to fry

MARINADE

2 tablespoons soy sauce
2 tablespoons rice syrup
(p. 24)
2 cloves of garlic,
minced
pinch of pepper
1 teaspoon toasted
sesame oil

PREPARATION

Soak the beef in cold water for 15 minutes. Take it out and rinse under cold running water. Pat dry with a kitchen towel or paper towel. Cut into fine slices a few millimetres thick. Mix all the ingredients for the marinade together and add the meat slices, leaving it preferably for at least 1 hour (the longer, the better). Finely chop the onion and spring onion. Heat a pan with oil, and fry everything together.

GOOD TO KNOW

*   Other flavourful tender beef cuts like sirloin or tenderloin are suitable too.

Bulgogi and other fried or grilled meats are often served in Korea with an assortment of *ssam* (see p. 167) and *ssamjang*, a sauce based on soybean and chilli paste. With each bite of meat, you also have your dose of fresh vegetables – a delicious combination.

파프리카 제육볶음

FRIED PORK MEDALLION WITH PEPPERS

INGREDIENTS

250g pork medallions
(pork belly or smelt)
¼ onion
1 red pepper
½ Spanish red chilli
pepper
½ Spanish green chilli
pepper
1 spring onion
1 tablespoon vegetable
oil, to fry

MARINADE

1 tablespoon chilli
paste
2 tablespoons soy sauce
1 tablespoon rice syrup
(see p. 24)
1 garlic clove, minced

PREPARATION

Make the marinade by mixing all the ingredients.
Marinate the pork medallions. Meanwhile, cut the
onion into 0.5cm half-moons. Remove the seeds from
the bell pepper and cut in a similar shape as the
onion. Chop the chilli peppers and spring onion
into fine diagonal rings. Heat oil in a pan and
stir fry everything together.

토마토카르파치오

TOMATO CARPACCIO

INGREDIENTS

2 beefsteak tomatoes
coarsely ground black
pepper
pinch of chilli powder

SAUCE

1.5 tablespoon soy sauce
1 tablespoon apple cider
vinegar
1 tablespoon cane sugar
1 tablespoon extra
virgin olive oil

PREPARATION

Rinse the tomatoes, remove the stems and cut into
fine slices with a razor-sharp knife or mandolin.
Make the sauce by mixing all the ingredients.
Arrange the tomato slices neatly on a flat plate,
pour the sauce over, and give it a twist of the
pepper mill. Add some chilli for a spicy touch.

PICKLED SALMON

INGREDIENTS

200g salmon tenderloin
½ onion
20 capers

BRINE WATER

8 tablespoons soy sauce
150ml water
1 tablespoon water
2 tablespoons natural
vinegar
1 teaspoon cane sugar
3 slices of ginger
½ Spanish chilli pepper,
finely chopped
2g kelp

PREPARATION

Cut the salmon into bite-sized pieces. Shred the onion. Make the brine by mixing the ingredients and bring to a boil. Let it cool. Take a mason jar, add the onion, capers, and salmon, and pour in the brine. Add the chilli pepper. Marinate for at least 4 hours before serving as a snack or topping with a rice bowl (see p. 41).

GOOD TO KNOW

The remaining brine can be kept in the refrigerator for another week. Delicious cold as a broth with boiled wheat noodles, but it can also serve as a base for various marinades or dipping sauces.

고구마 닭갈비

SWEET POTATO WITH CHICKEN

INGREDIENTS

400g chicken thigh
1 onion
¼ leek
vegetable oil, to fry
1 sweet potato
(150-200 g)
5 tablespoons water

SAUCE

2 tablespoons soy sauce
2 tablespoons chilli
powder
1 tablespoon rice syrup
(see p. 24)
2 cloves of garlic,
minced

PREPARATION

Mix the sauce ingredients in a jar. Separate the chicken meat from the bone and cut into bite-sized pieces. Rinse and peel the potato. Halve lengthwise and cut into half-moon slices of 0.5cm thick. Slice the leek and onion on a slant into oval discs of 0.5cm thick. Heat a dash of vegetable oil in a pan. Stir fry the chicken, potato, and onion together. If the bottom of the pan becomes too dry, turn down the heat. Add the sauce and rinse the sauce jar with 5 tablespoons of water. Add this liquid to the mix and stir fry until everything is cooked. Finally, mix in the leeks.

ROASTED PUMPKIN*

INGREDIENTS

1 spring pumpkin
an appropriate amount
of toasted sesame oil
(*sonmat*, see p. 20)
an appropriate amount of
soy sauce (*sonmat*, see
p. 20)
fresh pine twigs with
needles

PREPARATION

Cut the pumpkin into finger-thick moons. Rub the pumpkin with the mixture of soy sauce and sesame oil at 10-minute intervals so that the pumpkin absorbs the aromas optimally. Bake gently in a thick-bottomed frying pan at low temperature. Cut some tops off the pine twigs and push them diagonally into the pumpkin.

ORIGINAL RECIPE (IMWON GEYONGJEJI, JEONGJOJI)

Well kept, old, yellow pumpkins can still be used up until March of the following year. When the pine leaves produce new buds, you cut the pumpkin into finger-thick chunks. String these pieces together with pine branches and smear them with sesame oil and soy sauce. The sweet and fragrant flavours emanating when you bake this in an open fire are truly incomparable.

*   RECIPE TRANSLATED BY THE STUDY GROUP LED BY CHUNG CHUNG KEE
(see p. 196).

CARROT PANCAKE

INGREDIENTS

2 carrots with their greens
5 tablespoons potato starch
7 tablespoons wheat flour
5 tablespoons water
pinch of salt
vegetable oil, to fry

DIPPING SAUCE

1 tablespoon soy sauce
1 teaspoon natural vinegar
pinch of cane sugar
¼ Spanish chilli pepper (optional)

PREPARATION

Mix the ingredients to make the dipping sauce. Add finely chopped chilli pepper for a spicier version. Cut the greens from the carrots and rinse separately from the carrots. Drain the greens and julienne the carrots with a small knife or, alternatively, with a mandolin, papaya peeler, or julienne cutter. Coarsely chop the carrot greens. Make the pancake batter by mixing all the ingredients in a bowl. Heat a generous dash of vegetable oil in a pan. You can choose to bake one large pancake or several small ones. Flip the pancake only when the edges turn golden brown. Fry the other side until equally coloured. These pancakes are best served immediately, accompanied by the dipping sauce.

GOOD TO KNOW

Carrot greens are often discarded, which is a waste as the stems and leaves are perfectly edible and have a pleasantly subtle carrot flavour. They can also be a nice decoration to your dish.
Some kitchen chores go faster with specialist tools. A mandolin should be handled with care and a julienne cutter is a safe alternative for slicing vegetables. The Thai papaya peeler, found in most Asian supermarkets, gives a similar result.

BRAISED BABY POTATO AND CHESTNUT*

감자밤조림

INGREDIENTS

150g baby potatoes
5 to 10 sweet chestnuts
1 tablespoon vegetable
oil
1 tablespoon soy sauce
1.5 tablespoons rice
syrup (see p. 24)
1 teaspoon perilla oil
(see p. 119)
1 teaspoon grated ginger
1 teaspoon toasted
sesame seeds

PREPARATION

Pre-heat the oven to 180°C. Thoroughly rinse the baby potatoes and clean the chestnuts. Put the potatoes and chestnuts in an oven dish, mix with oil and cook them in the oven. Turn them frequently so they cook evenly. Check if they are done by piercing them with a fork or chopstick. Take the dish out of the oven and add soy sauce, rice syrup, perilla oil, and ginger. Finish with toasted sesame seeds.

GOOD TO KNOW

The original recipe by Wook Wan Seunim mentions potatoes and a pot on a heat source using a pot on a heat source. For convenience, I replaced plain potatoes with baby potatoes, as they are similar in size to chestnuts. I prefer to make this dish in an oven rather than a pot, which requires continuous stir frying for the potatoes to cook evenly.

*　　RECIPE BY WOOK WAN SEUNIM (see p. 17).

된
장
감
자
조
림

BRAISED POTATOES WITH SOYBEAN PASTE*

INGREDIENTS

6 potatoes
2 onions
½ litre water
6 tablespoons soybean
paste
4 tablespoons rice syrup
(see p. 24)
2 to 3 tablespoons
chilli powder
15 small, dried
anchovies

PREPARATION

Peel the vegetables and chop them into equal 1cm chunks. Arrange them in a casserole and add the remaining ingredients. Simmer with the lid on until the potatoes are cooked.

GOOD TO KNOW

For a vegan version of this recipe, you can leave out the dried anchovies (*myeolchi*).

* RECIPE BY KIM EUN YOUNG.

Chef Kim Eun Young and I had a few mutual acquaintances who wanted me to meet her. It seemed destined that our paths would cross. Then she invited me into her cosy kitchen, where we cooked together all day long. We scoured through all sorts of recipes and, conscious of her food philosophy, I chose to share this special recipe with you. It is a local recipe from Jeju Island – where Young grew up and still lives. Her mother gave it her own special *sonmat* twist (see p. 20).

We all have our own soul food. It is the food that makes you happy, the food that paints a smile on your face, the food that makes you sigh with satisfaction when you start eating. That is *your* specific soul food. If you respond strongly to taste, you may have several soul foods. Your soul does not mind the price, portion size, or nutritional value of the food. Transcending time and space, the taste and smell molecules of a meal stored in your memory may spark something inside. You might think you have forgotten, but your soul surely remembers.

– Kim Eun Young

PICKLED ONION

INGREDIENTS

2 onions (or fresh
silverskin onions)
1 Spanish green chilli
pepper

BRINE WATER

10ml soy sauce
200ml water
4 tablespoons natural
vinegar
1 teaspoon sugar

PREPARATION

Take two peeled onions and chop them coarsely or
opt for small peeled silverskin onions. Rinse the
chilli pepper and cut into fine rings. Put the
onion and chilli into a mason jar. Make the brine
water by mixing and boiling the ingredients. When
the boiling point is reached, pour the brine water
over the fresh vegetables and allow to cool. After
24 hours, drain the brine water into a pan, bring
it to the boil and pour it over the vegetables
a second time. Allow to cool and store in the
refrigerator. These pickled onions can be served
as a supplementary seasoning with various kinds of
dishes (see recipes p. 81, 135, 151, 157).

가리비샐러드

SCALLOP SALAD*

INGREDIENTS

3 fresh scallops
1 green melon
2 tablespoons extra
virgin olive oil
2 tablespoons yuja
mayonnaise (see p. 90)

PREPARATION

Cut the scallops into 0.5cm slices. Cut the melon
into fine 0.3mm slices and press out shapes with
the same diameter as your scallops. Build towers,
alternating between the melon and scallop chunks.
Finish with olive oil and yuja mayonnaise.

*   RECIPE BY KIM DO YUN.

YUJA MAYONNAISE*

유
자
마
여
내
스

INGREDIENTS

135g mirin**
45g Korean rice wine
450g soy sauce
450g yuja***
15g katsuobushi****
75g mayonnaise

PREPARATION

Put the mirin and rice wine in a cooking pot
and bring to the boil, then turn off the heat
and allow to cool. Next, add the remaining
ingredients, except for the mayonnaise. Pour the
mass into a jar, close, and leave to infuse in the
refrigerator for 7 days. You now have yuja soy
sauce. Mix this yuja soy sauce (135 grams) with
mayonnaise and you have yuja mayonnaise.

GOOD TO KNOW

*   RECIPE BY KIM DO YUN.
**   Japanese sweet rice wine.
***   Korean mandarin orange, similar to the Japanese *yuzu*.
**** Japanese bonito flakes, these are flakes of dried fermented smoked tuna.

죽장연된장페스토

JUKJANGYEON DOENJANG PESTO*

INGREDIENTS

35g Jukjangyeon premium
soybean paste**
50g pistachios
50g macadamia nuts
50g hazelnuts
40g salted anchovies,
canned
100g extra virgin olive
oil

PREPARATION

With a blender, puree all the ingredients together
to obtain a smooth paste. The texture of the
ground nuts should resemble coarsely ground coffee
beans.

GOOD TO KNOW

*   RECIPE BY KIM DO YUN.
**   A premium soybean paste from artisan producer Jukjangyeon (see p. 200)
      from the year 2012. This recipe is equally delicious with any other
      decent quality soybean paste.

Kim Do Yun exudes focus and dedication. Our paths crossed several times and, during my last trip to Korea, I learned that he had a brand-new Michelin star to his name. The restaurant at the centre of his universe bears the name 'Yun Seoul' and is hidden away in the busy student district of Hongik University in Hongdae. As befits any Michelin star holder, every single one of his dishes is a refined work of art, yet I was most in awe of his *doenjang pesto*. It reminded me of a quotation from my Korean friend, Go Young Joo (a Korean chocolatier who runs Cacaoboom): "Don't make new recipes if they're not better than the original." Making a fusion recipe with old traditional seasonings is no easy thing, but his pesto bowled me over as soon as it touched my tongue.

느
타
리
버
섯
죽

RICE PORRIDGE WITH OYSTER MUSHROOM

INGREDIENTS

100g Korean or Japanese sushi rice (round white grain)
150g oyster mushrooms
1 spring onion
600ml water
2g kelp
2 tablespoons soy sauce
pinch of ground black pepper
1 teaspoon toasted sesame oil

PREPARATION

Rinse the rice until the water turns clear. Drain well and let the rice rest for half an hour. Meanwhile, clean the vegetables: finely chop the oyster mushrooms, and slice the spring onion into thin rings. Bring the rice to a boil with the water and kelp. At first, stir the rice regularly so it doesn't stick to the bottom. When it comes to the boil, set the heat to low, and then add the oyster mushrooms and spring onion. Let it simmer for about 10 minutes or until the rice is overcooked and most of the moisture has evaporated. The desired consistency is that of a watery rice porridge. You can take out the kelp if you want. Season the juk (porridge) with soy sauce, pepper, and sesame oil.

연두부

SILKEN TOFU WITH SOY SAUCE

INGREDIENTS

1 packet of silken tofu
(200-300g)

MARINADE

1 tablespoon soy sauce
1 tablespoon perilla oil
(see p. 119)
¼ leek, chopped finely

PREPARATION

Remove the foil from the packet of silken tofu and allow any liquid to drain away. Put a plate upside down on top of the tofu. In one smooth movement, turn over the plate with the tofu so that the tofu drops from the package onto your plate. Make the marinade by mixing the ingredients and dress the tofu with it.

GOOD TO KNOW

In Korea, specialized eateries that fabricate fresh tofu are definitely worth a visit. You will find all kinds of soybean preparations on the menu: from freshly cooked soy milk, silky soft tofu that can be eaten with a spoon, and savoury soup of ground soybeans (*kongbiji*, a residue from making tofu) to pure tofu in combination with fermented cabbage (*dubu kimchi*).

두부구이

FRIED TOFU

INGREDIENTS

1 packet of firm tofu
(250-350g)
vegetable oil, to fry

SAUCE

4 tablespoons soy sauce
¼ leek, chopped very
thinly
2 tablespoons toasted
sesame oil
2 tablespoons toasted
sesame seeds

PREPARATION

Open the packet of tofu and let the liquid drain
off. Pat dry with a clean kitchen towel or paper
towel. Cut into bite-sized pieces about 1cm long.
Heat a generous dash of vegetable oil in a pan.
Fry the tofu until golden brown on both sides.
Make the sauce by mixing the ingredients and dress
the tofu.

GOOD TO KNOW

The type of tofu determines how it should be prepared. Tofu is classified
according to its moisture content and consistency. Silken tofu contains the
most moisture and is, as its name suggests, silky smooth. Firm tofu contains
the least moisture and is best pan fried or deep fried. The intermediate
type is typically added to stews or soups. Western supermarkets mainly sell
tofu with a hard and dry texture, hence best suited for pan frying or deep
frying. Asian supermarkets have a larger selection. Going from soft to firm,
the English descriptions on the labels will be: silken - regular - firm -
extra firm.

SPICY FISH SOUP

INGREDIENTS

100g daikon
¼ onion
3 slices of ginger
1 spring onion
5g kelp
250g cod (1 fillet)
½ Spanish red chilli
pepper (optional)
10 shellfish of your
choice, cleaned
(optional)

SAUCE

1 tablespoon soybean
paste
1 tablespoon chilli
paste
1 tablespoon soy sauce
1 tablespoon fish sauce
2 cloves of garlic,
crushed
300ml water

PREPARATION

Mix the ingredients for the sauce. Peel the daikon
and cut into 1cm crescents. Roughly chop the onion
and place in the bottom of your pot together with
the daikon, ginger, spring onion, and kelp. Put
the cod on top and add the sauce. Simmer gently
until everything is cooked. At the end, add the
shellfish to the soup and cook briefly until they
open.

고등어조림

STEWED MACKEREL

INGREDIENTS

1 1 fresh mackerel
(innards removed)
200g daikon
¼ onion
½ Spanish red chilli
pepper
5g kelp
2 cloves of garlic,
crushed or minced
1 thick slice of ginger
pinch of black pepper
¼ leek
4 tablespoons soy sauce
300ml water
1 tablespoon chilli
powder
pinch of sugar

PREPARATION

Remove the tail and fins from the mackerel. Divide
the fish into three equal portions. Rinse the
fish thoroughly, clearing excess blood clots.
Place the portions in a bath of water. Meanwhile,
peel the daikon and halve lengthwise. Cut into
1cm half-moons. Arrange them on the bottom of a
wide casserole together with the coarsely chopped
onion. Put the pieces of fish on top and add the
remaining ingredients, except the leeks. Bring to
a gentle boil, spooning the broth over the fish to
make sure it is completely covered. Let it simmer
until everything is cooked. Finally, add in the
finely chopped leek.

홍합 된장찜

STEAMED MUSSELS WITH DOENJANG

INGREDIENTS

250g Bouchot mussels,
cleaned

SAUCE

1 tablespoon soybean
paste
1 garlic clove, minced
200ml water
5g kelp
pinch of salt

PREPARATION

Put a pan on the stove and heat the sauce, making
sure the soybean paste dissolves nicely. Then
add the mussels and wait until they open. Serve
directly as a snack, soup, or sharing dish.

가
지
찜

STEAMED AUBERGINE

INGREDIENTS

2 thin aubergines
2 spring onions or a
bunch of chives

SAUCE

2 tablespoons soy sauce
1 garlic clove, minced
1 tablespoon perilla oil
(see p. 119)
½ teaspoon chilli powder
1 tablespoon toasted
sesame seeds

PREPARATION

Mix the ingredients for the sauce. Steam or grill
the whole aubergines until tender. Prick with a
skewer in the centre. If the skewer enters easily,
the aubergines are cooked. Slice them into 4cm-
thick rings and carve a 2.5cm-deep cross in the
centre. Drain briefly in a colander. Arrange the
aubergine on a plate, and finish with the sauce.

고추장가지덮밥

AUBERGINE WITH CHILLI PASTE AND RICE*

INGREDIENTS

2 aubergines
rice bran oil, to fry
150g cooked rice (see
p.41)

SAUCE

2 tablespoons chilli
paste
1.5 tablespoons soy
sauce
1.5 tablespoons
muscovado sugar
1 tablespoon red chilli
oil
2 tablespoons chopped
ginger

PREPARATION

Halve the aubergines lengthwise. Cut long
indentations in the flesh up to where the stem
starts, paying attention not to slice through the
skin. Heat some rice bran oil in a pan and fry the
aubergines until golden brown. Mix the ingredients
for the sauce and add when the liquid in the
aubergines has evaporated sufficiently. Simmer
until the aubergines are cooked. Put the boiled
rice in a bowl and arrange the aubergines on top.

---

*   RECIPE BY MOON SUN HEE (see p. 33).

적양배추회덮밥

RICE BOWL WITH RED CABBAGE AND RAW FISH

INGREDIENTS

100g red cabbage
100g sea bass fillet,
skinned
1 teaspoon toasted
sesame oil
50g pea shoots (or other
sprouts of your choice)
150g boiled rice (see
p. 41)

BRINE WATER

100ml apple cider
vinegar
100ml water
4 tablespoons sugar

SAUCE

1 tablespoon chilli
paste
1 tablespoon apple cider
vinegar
1 tablespoon rice syrup
(see p. 24)
1 garlic clove, minced
1 teaspoon toasted
sesame seeds

PREPARATION

Remove the cabbage core and outer leaves. Finely
slice the remainder – you can get it wafer-thin
with a mandolin. Put the shredded cabbage into a
mason jar. Prepare the brine water, bring to the
boil, and pour over the cabbage. Leave to cool.
Do this at least 4 hours in advance, or the day
before if possible.
Cut the sea bass into fine 0.5cm pieces. Drizzle
the sesame oil over the fish. Now make the sauce
by mixing all the ingredients. Squeeze the liquid
out of the pickled red cabbage and drain. Put the
boiled rice in a bowl and arrange the sprouts, red
cabbage and fish with some spoonfuls of sauce on
top. Mix everything together before serving with
the rice.

GOOD TO KNOW

To brine an entire cabbage, adjust the amount of water, vinegar, and sugar
accordingly. Pickled cabbage has a long shelf life and retains its nice
fresh taste if you keep it in the fridge.
For a vegan version of this dish, you can leave out the fish and replace it
with more sprouts.

SEASONED LETTUCE FLOWER STALKS*

INGREDIENTS

lettuce flower stalks**
2 shiitakes
1 tablespoon pine nuts
1 tablespoon soy sauce
1 teaspoon toasted
sesame oil

PREPARATION

Briefly blanch the lettuce flower stalks in
boiling water to remove the hard exterior, then
chop into 3 to 3.5cm pieces. Chop the shiitakes
similarly to the lettuce flower stalks. Rinse the
pine nuts, remove the brown ends (optional)*** and
chop finely. Mix the soy sauce and sesame oil in
a pan, add the lettuce flower stalks and shredded
shiitakes, stir fry and arrange in a bowl. Scatter
the finely ground pine nuts over it.

GOOD TO KNOW

The word *namul* refers to edible greenery (plants or leaves), frequently
flavoured with jang. *Namul* is associated with picking in the wild and with
times when people suffering food shortages went foraging for plants in
fields and mountainous areas.

ORIGINAL RECIPE (*Imwon Geyongjeji, Jeongjoji*)

Boil the tender lettuce flower stalks in water, peel them and cut into
pieces of 0.1 *cheok*****. Pour oil and soy sauce into a heated pot and
blanch the lettuce flower stalks. Add ear mushrooms, mago (wild shiitakes),
shiitakes, and ground pine nuts and stir fry everything together in a pan.

*   RECIPE TRANSLATED BY THE STUDY GROUP LED BY CHUNG KEE (see p. 196).

**   When lettuce bolts, the heart of the head produces a thick upward stalk
       with seeds, eventually forming flower buds.
***   Koreans remove the brown ends of pine nuts (by pinching the tip) for
       aesthetic reasons.
**** 1 *cheok* = 30.3cm (Korean measurement unit)

PRAWN PANCAKE

INGREDIENTS

6 large prawns
1 egg
wheat flour, to dust
vegetable oil, to fry

DIPPING SAUCE

1 tablespoon soy sauce
1 tablespoon apple cider
vinegar
1 tablespoon yellow
mustard

PREPARATION

Peel the prawns and remove the heads (the tails can stay). Put the prawns on the cutting board and cut along the length of the back to remove the intestinal tract. Press the prawns somewhat to flatten, and dust them with flour. Turn them over and dust the other side. Beat the egg and dip the prawns in the mix. Put the heat on low and, in an oiled pan, fry the prawns lightly on both sides. Make sure the egg yolk stays nice and yellow – not golden brown. Make the dipping sauce by mixing all the ingredients and serve the prawn pancakes with the sauce.

GOOD TO KNOW

For bites that look even more inviting, add finely chopped vegetables to the egg mix.

돼지감자장아찌

PICKLED JERUSALEM ARTICHOKE*

INGREDIENTS

500g Jerusalem artichoke

BRINE WATER

100ml water
100ml soy sauce
50ml apple cider vinegar
50ml rice syrup
(see p. 24)

PREPARATION

Thoroughly rinse the artichoke and drain in a
sieve. Place it in a 1.5-litre mason jar. Boil
the brine, skim off any scum. Pour the hot brine
over the artichoke in the jar and allow to cool.
Repeat this process the following day: pour the
brine from the jar into a pan, bring to the boil
and pour over the artichoke in the jar. Let it
cool. Store at room temperature or else in the
refrigerator if you prefer a chilled dish.

* RECIPE BY WOOK WAN SEUNIM (see p. 17).

BUCKWHEAT NOODLES WITH PERILLA OIL

INGREDIENTS

100g buckwheat noodles
1 teaspoon toasted
sesame seeds
½ seaweed sheet,
preferably toasted

SAUCE

1 tablespoon soy sauce
1 tablespoon perilla oil

PREPARATION

Cook the noodles al dente for 4 to 5 minutes
(depending on brand and type). Keep a jug of
water at hand to add a splash of cold water to
the cooking liquid, which will quickly rise.
Repeat this a couple of times until the noodles
are cooked. Rinse them quickly in cold running
water and drain briefly. Make the sauce by mixing
the ingredients. Add the sauce to the noodles and
finish with crumbled seaweed and sesame seeds.

GOOD TO KNOW

깻잎 *kaennip* is the Korean name for perilla (*perilla frutescens*), which
originated in East Asia and is related to mint. Perilla is widely used
in Korean cuisine. The leaf is delicious as a salad or added to various
preparations. In Korean, the seeds are called *deulkkae* and the ground seeds
deulkkaegaru. The oil that is pressed from these seeds, *deulkireum*, is
(together with toasted sesame oil) the main oil for flavouring dishes. In
the West, perilla is more commonly found in medicines or supplements than
in cooking due to its medicinal properties. The Japanese variant is better
known as *shiso*. Perilla oil can be found in most Korean supermarkets, and
toasted sesame oil is the most commonly used alternative.
Seaweed paper can be toasted in a pan in just a few seconds. Be careful
and do it quickly: take the seaweed out of the pan as soon as the colour
changes. You can also buy toasted seaweed; this variant is brushed with oil
and slightly salted. Once toasted, you can just crumble the seaweed paper
with your hands.

새
송
이
강
정

SWEET FRIED ERYNGII

INGREDIENTS

2 large eryngii
(mushrooms)
wheat flour, to dust
vegetable oil, to pan
fry or deep fry

BATTER

5 tablespoons potato
starch
5 tablespoons wheat
flour
15 tablespoons cold
water

SAUCE

3 tablespoons chilli
paste
2 tablespoons rice syrup
(see p. 24)
6 tablespoons water
1 garlic clove, minced

PREPARATION

Cut the eryngii into equal bite-sized pieces. Dust
the pieces with flour and shake off any excess.
Take a bowl and make the batter by mixing the
ingredients. Meanwhile, make sure the fryer oil is
brought up to temperature or prepare your pan with
a generous amount of oil. Dip the eryngii pieces
one by one in the batter and fry until they turn
light brown. Drain off the excess oil in the fryer
or with paper towels in a platter. Make the sauce
by mixing all the ingredients in a saucepan and
heat it up. Coat the eryngii with the sauce.

GOOD TO KNOW

You can replace the eryngii with other sorts of mushrooms, chicken, tofu or
cauliflower. For a super crispy version, use more starch than flour, and
fry the eryngii twice before covering them with the sauce. This dish is also
delicious chilled.

표고버섯청국장찌개

STEW OF SHIITAKE WITH FAST FERMENTED SOYBEAN PASTE

INGREDIENTS

½ packet of tofu (100-150g)
10 shiitakes
500ml water
½ onion, shredded
1 to 2 garlic cloves to taste, minced
150g fast fermented soybean paste (cheonggukjang, (see p. 24, 193)
1 to 2 tablespoons chilli powder (to your own taste)
¼ Spanish red chilli pepper
¼ Spanish green chilli pepper
pinch of salt
pinch of black pepper

PREPARATION

Drain the tofu. Remove the shiitake stems and set the mushrooms aside. Bring the water to a boil together with the shiitake stems, onion, garlic, soybean paste and chilli powder. Break the shiitake caps with your hands into bite-sized pieces into the cooking pot. Do the same with the tofu. Cut the chilli peppers into fine diagonal slices and add these at the end. Cook until everything is done and bring up to taste with some salt and pepper if needed.

서양우엉조림

BRAISED SALSIFY

INGREDIENTS

200g salsify
1 teaspoon natural
vinegar
vegetable oil, to fry

SAUCE

1 tablespoon chilli
paste
2 tablespoons soy sauce
2 tablespoons water
1 tablespoon rice syrup
(see p. 24)
1 garlic clove, minced

PREPARATION

Peel the salsify under water, rinse thoroughly
until they are nice and white. Put them in
a fresh water bath with vinegar to prevent
discolouration. Halve the salsify lengthwise,
crush with a rolling pin and cut into bite-
sized 4cm pieces. Add some oil to a pan and
fry briefly. Make the sauce by mixing all the
ingredients and add to the pan. Stir fry until
the salsify is al dente, or longer for a softer
texture. Personally, I like them slightly
crispy.

미역국

SEAWEED SOUP

INGREDIENTS

10g wakame
2 cloves of garlic, pureed
1 tablespoon toasted sesame oil
1 tablespoon soy sauce
500ml water
1 teaspoon fish sauce (optional)
pinch of salt

PREPARATION

Soak the wakame for about half an hour in plenty of water. Drain and cut into bite-sized portions. Stew the garlic and seaweed with oil and soy sauce, then add 500ml of water. Bring to the boil and season with fish sauce and/or a pinch of salt for a fuller taste.

GOOD TO KNOW

Seaweed is one of my favourite ingredients and, since South Korea is a peninsula, it is a mecca for lovers of fish and sea vegetables. Seaweed comes in countless shapes and sizes and has at least as many applications in Korean cuisine. In particular, the dish *miyeok guk* has earned a special place in Korean food culture. This seaweed soup has been served to new mothers for centuries, because the quantities of calcium and iron present in seaweed promote blood circulation. Seafood or beef are often added for extra protein. Eating seaweed soup on your birthday has been an annual tradition in Korea since time immemorial as a kind of tribute to your mother. In Western countries, the use of seaweed is slowly on the rise. Since seaweed can be found on every coastline, has significant health benefits, and is grown sustainably, it is often called the vegetable of the future.

STUFFED SAVOY CABBAGE ROLLS

INGREDIENTS

1 savoy cabbage (15 leaves)
250g minced pork
½ onion, finely chopped
½ bunch of chives, finely chopped
1 tablespoon grated ginger
1 garlic clove, minced
1 tablespoon toasted sesame oil
pinch of pepper

DIPPING SAUCE

1 tablespoon soy sauce
1 tablespoon water
1 teaspoon natural vinegar
1 teaspoon toasted sesame oil
1 teaspoon toasted sesame seeds (optional)
pinch of chilli powder (optional)

PREPARATION

Remove the outer leaves from the cabbage, and carefully separate the remaining leaves. Cut out the central stem to obtain two leaf halves. Wash the leaves thoroughly and steam or boil them for a few minutes until they can be easily folded. Drain and cool in a sieve. Meanwhile, mix all the ingredients for the filling. To make the rolls, put a full tablespoon of minced meat on each cabbage leaf. Roll them into equal packages. Steam for 10 minutes. Cut a roll in half to check if cooked. If not, cook for another 5 minutes. Make the dipping sauce by mixing all the ingredients and serve the cabbage rolls with this dip.

GOOD TO KNOW

You can also grill the rolls in the oven or in a pan. In that case, grease them all over with vegetable oil and turn the rolls occasionally to fry evenly.

STEAMED BROCCOLI

INGREDIENTS

1 broccoli

DIPPING SAUCE

1 tablespoon chilli paste
2 tablespoons soybean
paste
1 tablespoon rice syrup
(see p. 24)
1 garlic clove, minced
1 teaspoon of water

PREPARATION

Mix the ingredients for the dipping sauce. Rinse the broccoli and divide into long broccoli florets. Steam the florets until they are al dente. Serve with the dipping sauce as a snack or as a vegetable side dish.

GOOD TO KNOW

Feel free to replace the broccoli by other vegetables like leek, cauliflower, asparagus...

시
금
치
나
물

SEASONED SPINACH

INGREDIENTS

200g spinach
ice cubes (optional)
pinch of salt (optional)

SAUCE

1 tablespoon soybean
paste
1 garlic clove, minced
1 teaspoon toasted
sesame oil
1 teaspoon toasted
sesame seeds

PREPARATION

Bring the water to the boil and turn off the heat.
Blanch the spinach for a few seconds, then quickly
transfer the spinach to a bowl of cold water with
ice cubes (or rinse under cold running water).
Squeeze out as much excess water as possible
without bruising the spinach. The net weight
should now be 100 grams. Cut the spinach into
bite-sized strips. Make the sauce by mixing all
the ingredients and stir well into the spinach.
Add a pinch of salt if desired.

케일장떡

KALE PANCAKE WITH FERMENTED SAUCE

INGREDIENTS

50g kale (3 leaves)
vegetable oil, to fry

BATTER

50g wheat flour
50g corn or potato
starch
1 tablespoon soybean
paste
1 teaspoon chilli paste
100ml water
½ onion, finely chopped
½ Spanish red chilli
pepper, finely chopped

PREPARATION

Peel off the cabbage leaves. Make the batter
by mixing the batter ingredients, then add the
shredded leaves. Heat some vegetable oil in a pan
and fry one large or several small pancakes until
crispy on both sides.

GOOD TO KNOW

You can replace the kale with another vegetable or a mixture. The
characteristic taste of this dish stems from the *jang* (see p. 22). For a
more Western variant, *jangtteok* is also delicious as a vegetable burger with
some homemade mayonnaise.

CRISPY FRIED KALE

INGREDIENTS

3 kale leaves
wheat flour, to dust
vegetable oil, to fry
(in a pan or deep fryer)

BATTER

5 tablespoons water
50g corn or potato
starch
3 tablespoons wheat
flour

DIPPING SAUCE

2 tablespoons soy sauce
1 teaspoon vinegar
2 tablespoons water

PREPARATION

Wash the cabbage leaves and pat lightly dry with
a kitchen towel. Dust the leaves on both sides
with some wheat flour and then shake off the
excess flour. Prepare the batter by mixing the
ingredients. Give the leaves a good covering of
batter. Fry until crispy - this does not take
long. Watch out for spattering when the leaves are
put into the oil. Make the dipping sauce by mixing
the ingredients and serve with the fried kale.

CHERVIL SOUP

INGREDIENTS

small bunch of chervil
¼ onion
1 tablespoon vegetable oil, to fry
500ml water
3 tablespoons soy sauce

PREPARATION

Rinse the chervil thoroughly and remove only the wilted parts. Pat dry and chop finely. Cut the onion into small pieces and sauté in the oil until translucent. Now add the chervil and water. Cook until done, season with soy sauce, and puree finely with a blender.

GOOD TO KNOW

Chervil is virtually unknown in Korea. I regard this herb as the West's answer to aromatic Korean herbs like *minari*, *naenggi*, and *ssuk*. Especially in spring, various dishes are garnished with these spring herbs. Chervil, with its delicate aroma, has a wide range of uses. Roman chervil is a fantastic variety that can be picked in the wild.

처
빌
주
먹
밥

CHERVIL RICE BALLS

INGREDIENTS

small bunch of chervil
150g cooked rice
1 tablespoon toasted
sesame oil
1 teaspoon toasted
sesame seeds
soybean paste, as
topping

PREPARATION

Rinse the chervil thoroughly and remove only the wilted parts. Pat dry and chop very finely. Season the warm rice with the sesame oil and seeds, mixing in the finely chopped chervil. Make bite-sized balls and spread some soybean paste on each rice ball.

PICKLED BEAN LEAVES WITH SOYBEAN PASTE

INGREDIENTS

100g bean leaves
1 Spanish red chilli
pepper, finely chopped
pinch of salt

BRINE SAUCE

3 tablespoons soybean
paste
1 tablespoon apple cider
vinegar
2 tablespoons chilli
powder
1 onion, shredded
1 garlic clove, minced
100ml water

PREPARATION

Rinse the bean leaves and drain. Take a large bowl of water and dissolve a pinch of salt in it. Place the bean leaves in the salt bath for 1 minute, remove the water, and drain the leaves well in a sieve. Put all the ingredients for the brine sauce together in a bowl and puree finely with a blender. Add the finely chopped chilli pepper. Brush the leaves with the brine sauce and store in a sealed container in the refrigerator. This way they can keep for months. Serve these bean leaves as ssam (see p. 167) with rice or meat.

GOOD TO KNOW

The bean leaves can be replaced by leaves of Jerusalem artichoke, green beans...

An alternative recipe for brine: take 100ml water, 50ml soy sauce, 50ml apple cider vinegar and 1 tablespoon brown sugar. Mix all these ingredients until all sugar has dissolved, then soak the vegetables in the brine.

According to a Korean saying, Koreans consume consume all sorts of edible greens. This *zero-waste* attitude dates back to a past when Koreans had to be creative with what little there was. That time is long gone, but the knowledge and habits have remained. For instance, bean leaves in season are also served fresh as ssam (see p. 167).

오이비빔국수

COLD WHEAT NOODLES WITH CUCUMBER

INGREDIENTS

1 cucumber
120g wheat noodles

SAUCE

3 tablespoons chilli
paste
3 tablespoons rice syrup
(see p. 24)
1 tablespoon apple cider
vinegar
1 teaspoon toasted
sesame oil
1 tablespoon toasted
sesame seeds

PREPARATION

Rinse the cucumber and trim the ends. Cut the
cucumber into julienne strips (use a mandolin or
julienne cutter for convenience). Cook the noodles
until tender, and rinse under cold running water.
Drain.
Make the sauce by mixing all the ingredients. Mix
the noodles with the sauce and serve in a bowl.
Top with lots of cucumber strips and add the
remaining cucumber halfway through the meal.

CUCUMBER SALAD

INGREDIENTS

2 thin cucumbers (200 g)

SAUCE

1 tablespoon soy sauce
½ garlic clove
pinch of sugar
½ tablespoon chilli
powder (optional)
1 tablespoon toasted
sesame oil
1 tablespoon toasted
sesame seeds

PREPARATION

Rinse the cucumbers, halve them lengthwise. Cut
diagonally into fine slices up to 0.5cm thick.
Make the sauce by mixing all the ingredients.
Mix the cucumber with the sauce. This cucumber
salad is delicious as a side dish or on a savoury
sandwich.

고깔양배추구이

GRILLED POINTED CABBAGE

INGREDIENTS

1 pointed cabbage

SAUCE

8 tablespoons soy sauce
8 tablespoons vegetable
oil
5 cloves of garlic,
minced

PREPARATION

Preheat the oven to 180 °C. Remove the outer leaves of the cabbage and cut into quarters. Diagonally carve out the hard core, making sure the leaves stay connected. Arrange the cabbage wedges in a baking dish with the insides facing up. Combine all sauce ingredients and sprinkle this over the cabbage wedges. Roast in a preheated oven for 30 minutes or, depending on your oven, until the top turns dark and the cabbage is cooked al dente.

GOOD TO KNOW

It wasn't until I delved into Korean cuisine that I discovered that cabbage is some sort of superfood. Cabbage is often rich in minerals and vitamins and research even attributes antibacterial and antiviral properties to them. The vitamin C content in cabbages is even higher than in oranges. Korean cuisine has countless cabbage recipes. In addition to kimchi (fermented vegetables), there are plenty of other preparations that are equally healthy and tasty.

새
우
파
전

PRAWN PANCAKE WITH SPRING ONION

INGREDIENTS

1 to 2 spring onions
150g large prawns
½ Spanish red chilli
pepper, finely chopped
vegetable oil, to fry

BATTER

3 tablespoons wheat
flour
3 tablespoons potato
starch
2 tablespoons water

DIPPING SAUCE

See recipe for 'pickled
onion' (p. 87).

PREPARATION

Cut the spring onions into diagonal 1cm pieces.
Peel the prawns, remove the intestinal tracts and
cut into bite-sized pieces. Make the batter by
combining all the ingredients, then mix it with
the spring onions, chilli pepper, and prawns. In a
hot pan with a generous splash of vegetable oil,
fry the pancakes on one side until the edges turn
golden brown. Then flip and bake on the other side
until golden brown. Serve with the pickled onion
sauce to give each bite a fresh, spicy twist.

PICKLED WILD GARLIC

INGREDIENTS

500g wild garlic

BRINE WATER

200ml soy sauce
200 ml natural vinegar
100ml water
100g sugar
5g kelp (optional)
2 dried shiitakes
(optional)

PREPARATION

Rinse the wild garlic until it is clean and get rid of any damaged parts. Drain and place in a sufficiently deep dish. Make the brine by mixing the ingredients and bring it to the boil. Turn off the heat when it boils and pour it over the wild garlic. If needed, turn the wild garlic so that all leaves are submerged. Allow to cool completely. Collect the brine water in the pan, bring it once again to boiling point and pour over the garlic. Transfer the freshly pickled wild garlic into a sealable pot, making sure that it stays submerged (if necessary, use a weight). Store in the refrigerator.

GOOD TO KNOW

Pickled wild garlic is often served with pork. You can make a large quantity of this dish in one go when wild garlic is in season. That way you can enjoy it all year long, or as long as your stock lasts.

펜넬무침

FENNEL SALAD

INGREDIENTS

1 fennel bulb (200g)

SAUCE

2 tablespoons chilli
paste
1 teaspoon soy sauce
2 tablespoons rice syrup
(see p. 24)
2 tablespoons apple
cider vinegar
2 cloves of garlic,
minced
1 teaspoon chilli powder
(optional)
1 teaspoon toasted
sesame seeds (optional)
fresh fennel leaves
(optional)

PREPARATION

Slice the fennel paper-thin with a mandolin. Make
the sauce by mixing the ingredients. Stir the
fennel into the sauce and preferably let it stand
for an hour. Finish with chilli powder for a spicy
version and garnish with toasted sesame seeds or
fresh fennel leaves.

애
호
박
전

COURGETTE PANCAKE

INGREDIENTS

1 courgette
wheat flour, to dust
2 eggs, beaten
vegetable oil, to fry

DIPPING SAUCE

1 tablespoon soy sauce
1.5 tablespoons water
1 teaspoon natural
vinegar

PREPARATION

Mix the ingredients for the dipping sauce. Cut the courgette into 0.5cm slices and dip these in the flour. Shake off any excess flour and dip each slice in the beaten egg. Pan fry the slices in oil on both sides until golden brown. Whisk to combine the ingredients for the dipping sauce and serve with the pancakes.

아스파라거스소고기산적

ASPARAGUS BEEF SATAY*

INGREDIENTS

100g bullet steak
(round steak)
4 to 5 spears of
asparagus
pinch of salt
some pine nuts

BEEF MARINADE

1 garlic clove, chopped
1 tablespoon pear juice
2 tablespoons soy sauce
1 tablespoon sugar
1 tablespoon rice wine
1 tablespoon toasted
sesame oil
pinch of ground pepper

PREPARATION

Thoroughly combine all the marinade ingredients.
Cut the beef into 2 to 3cm-wide and 10cm-long
pieces and marinate for at least 30 minutes. Wash
the asparagus thoroughly under cold running water.
Peel them, remove the hard bottom, and cut them
into two pieces. Blanch the asparagus in boiling
water for 30 to 40 seconds with a pinch of salt.
Fry the beef evenly in a frying pan on medium
heat. Mount the pieces on the skewers, alternating
between beef and asparagus. Serve on a plate and
dress with the finely ground pine nuts.

*   RECIPE BY JANG BO HYUN.

Bo Hyun is a writer and lives with her husband and photographer, Zin Ho, in one of my favourite neighbourhoods in Seoul, Tongin-dong. They live in an old *hanok** and use their home as the setting for the photos in the cookbooks they create together. Bo Hyun handles the food styling with the sensitivity of an artist. When I worked with them on my two cookbooks in Korea and Belgium, we functioned like a well-oiled team.

When the asparagus appears, spring is in full swing, and summer is on its way. In this lush season full of abundance, asparagus tantalizes the taste buds with its sweet savour and crunchy texture. When paired with tasty, savoury beef, the culinary delight is twice as great.

– Jang Bo Hyun

GOOD TO KNOW

*   A hanok is a traditional house built according to the precepts of Korean architecture, including the principle that a house is best positioned with a mountain at the back and a river at the front.

꽈리고추찜

STEAMED SHISHITO PEPPERS

INGREDIENTS

100g shishito peppers
wheat flour, to dust

SAUCE

1 teaspoon soy sauce
1 teaspoon soybean paste
1 teaspoon rice syrup
(see p. 24)
1 teaspoon chilli powder
1 garlic clove, minced
1 teaspoon toasted
sesame oil
1 teaspoon toasted
sesame seeds

PREPARATION

Rinse the shishito peppers and remove the
stems. Dust the moist peppers with flour. Put
a cheesecloth in a steam basket and place the
floured peppers in the basket. Steam for 6 minutes
or until al dente. Make the sauce by mixing all
the ingredients and gently stir in the peppers.

GOOD TO KNOW

Chilli peppers exist in thousands of varieties, from very spicy to sweet
and mild. For this dish, you may use the mild variant. The shishito can be
replaced by jalapeño, kil sivri, padron, or other mild varieties.

대
파
무
침

LEEK SALAD

INGREDIENTS

1 thin leek

SAUCE

2 tablespoons soy sauce
1 tablespoon brown sugar
1 tablespoon apple cider
vinegar
½ teaspoon chilli powder
½ teaspoon toasted
sesame seeds

PREPARATION

Remove the root end of the leek and the dried green parts. Rinse the rest thoroughly and pat dry with a clean kitchen towel. Slice the leek into wafer-thin julienne strips. Thoroughly mix all the condiments to make the sauce and drizzle this over the leek before serving.

GOOD TO KNOW

This leek salad tastes delicious with a mouthful of fish or meat, but also in ssam (see p. 167) with a mouthful of rice.

WHITE CABBAGE WRAP

INGREDIENTS

¼ white cabbage

SAUCE

2 tablespoons soybean paste
1 teaspoon chilli paste
2 tablespoons rice syrup (see p. 24)
1 garlic clove, minced
1 shallot, finely chopped
1 spring onion
1 teaspoon toasted sesame oil

PREPARATION

Cut the white cabbage so that you only have the thin leaves left. Steam or boil these until tender. Meanwhile, make the sauce by mixing all the ingredients. Serve the steamed leaves on a plate, along with a pot of sauce and a bowl of cooked rice (see p. 41) and make savoury packets. To substitute the sauce, pure soybean paste or chilli paste can be added to taste.

GOOD TO KNOW

'쌈' refers to the Korean way of wrapping food. The wrap can be made from anything 'wrappable', such as seaweed, lettuce, boiled leaves, pickled greens, or fermented cabbage.
The wrap is filled with meat, fish, rice or a mix, and can have *jang* as an extra seasoning. What is great about the Korean *ssam* is that you can combine packages at the table to your own liking. *Yangbaechu ssam* is particularly delicious in its simplicity, and the fermented seasonings are the icing on the cake.

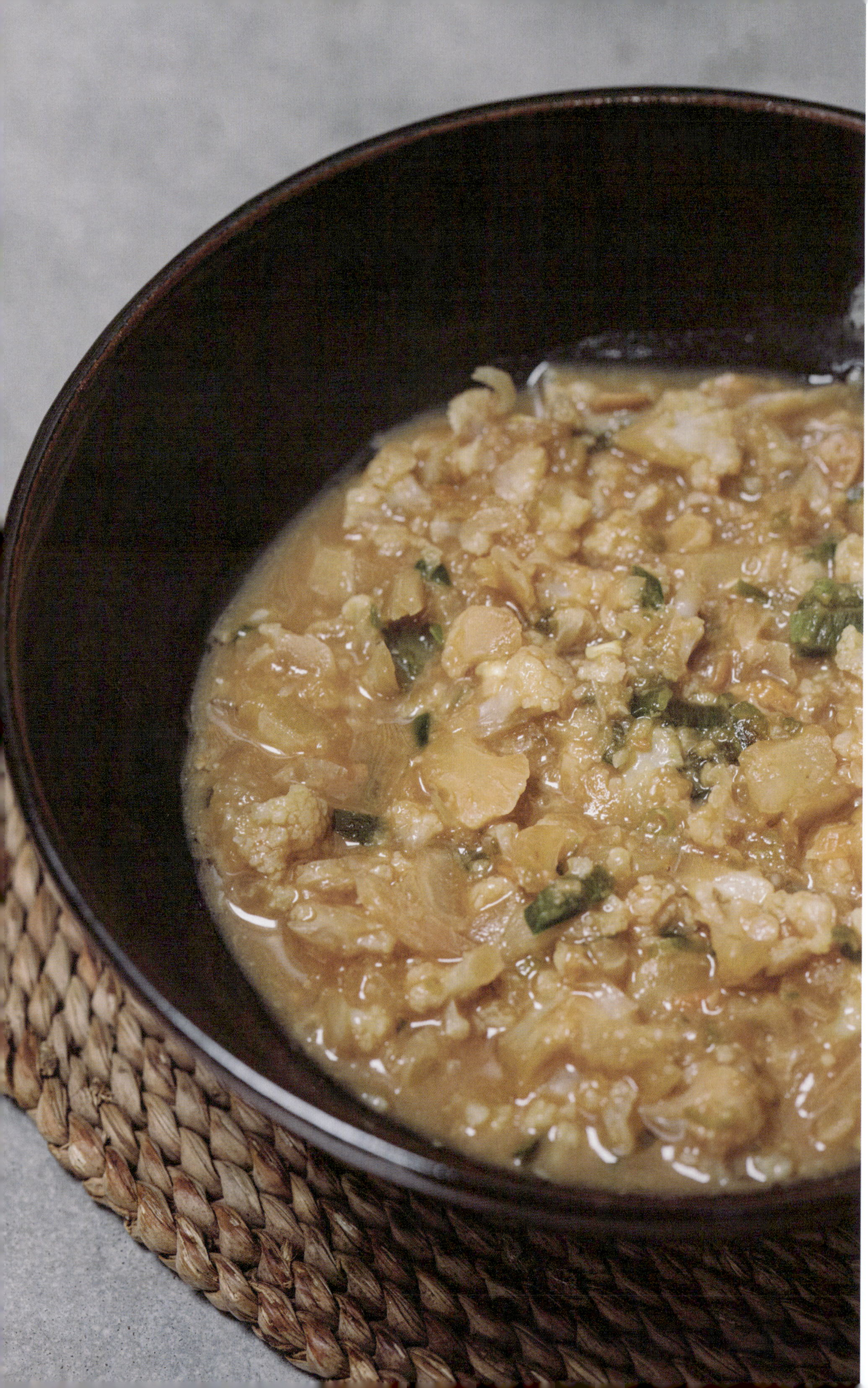

콜리플라워강된장

CAULIFLOWER WITH SOYBEAN PASTE

INGREDIENTS

500g cauliflower
5 tablespoons soybean
paste
150ml water
4 cloves of garlic,
minced
1 to 2 Spanish green
chilli peppers, finely
chopped

PREPARATION

Rinse the cauliflower, remove the bottom, and chop finely into 1cm square pieces. Put a pan of water on the heat and melt the soybean paste. Add the remaining ingredients. Simmer gently until everything is cooked. Serve as a savoury vegetable sauce with rice (see p. 41) or cooked grains. Very delicious too as a dip with crackers or toast.

SOY
— A VALUABLE CROP

The soybean, a legume originating from the subtropical soy plant (*Glycine max*), has a substantial economic value. For instance, soybean oil is the most intensely consumed vegetable oil worldwide after palm oil, and soy is one of the most important plant protein sources for human and animal consumption. At present, the vast majority of our soy is imported from South American countries for processing into animal feed. Unfortunately, the cultivation of soy in these countries is tainted by extensive logging. Nevertheless, soy cultivation for human consumption has some important benefits. For example, the soybean has a high protein content, making it an ideal meat substitute. It is essential to decrease our meat consumption in order to reduce our ecological footprint and the increasing pressure on our planet. By growing soy for human consumption locally, we can reduce our impact on the climate and, at the same time, offer our farmers an alternative crop in the current context of climate change.

SOY
— A SUSTAINABLE CROP

Additional research is needed to develop soy cultivation in Belgium with an acceptable yield. We must, therefore, delve into the biology of the soy plant, which, like many other legumes, uses an ingenious system. The soy plant collaborates with certain soil bacteria, called rhizobia, which can fixate nitrogen from the air. Through the root nodules in which these bacteria live, the rhizobia give this nitrogen to the plant in exchange for sugars. All plants need nitrogen to grow properly. In order to optimize crop yield, nitrogen fertilization is frequently used. However, this is detrimental to our soil and our climate. Since soy plants can meet their own nitrogen needs, they can grow on low nitrogen soils without the need for additional fertilizers. In fact, they add their own nitrogen to the soil. Growing soy, therefore, improves soil quality and reduces nitrogen pollution. This is an added benefit of local soy cultivation and makes soy a very sustainable crop.

INTRODUCING SOY INTO FLANDERS

It is crucial to map out which bacterial species in our soils work well with soy. After all, soy is a subtropical plant that is not adapted to our environment. If we want to tackle this, we must not only adjust the soy plant itself to our colder climate but also find the right local "partners" to absorb nitrogen for the soy plant in our soil. In this way, we can grow a protein-rich crop locally and sustainably, while simultaneously halting overfertilization with nitrogen fertilizers and improving soil quality.

SOY AS A SUSTAINABLE AGRICULTURAL CROP IN FLANDERS

In the long term, this project aims to enable Flemish farmers to grow soy in an economically viable way. This can be done, for example, by developing adapted seeds (with coatings of bacteria around the soy seeds) based on the data from this project. In this way, the required bacteria are immediately present and can fix nitrogen for the soy plant. By establishing collaborations with companies, these seeds can then be brought to the market. Thanks to this project, it may be possible to introduce protein-rich soy locally as a sustainable agricultural crop in the future.

SOY IN 1000 GARDENS

To bolster research into soy, the "Soy in 1000 Gardens" project was set up in 2021 as part of the VIB Grand Challenges Programme*. With the help of more than 1000 citizen scientists throughout Flanders, including dozens of farmers, the researchers in this project investigated which local bacterial species are good partners for soy. As a first step, the citizen scientists grew soy in their own gardens. The bacteria, soil samples, and soy plants from their gardens are currently being investigated in the lab. Based on the collected data on soil texture, management, nutrient composition, and the diversity of soil bacteria, we are learning more about the optimal conditions for growing soy locally. This knowledge can then be translated into guidelines for farmers to optimize local soy cultivation.

GOOD TO KNOW

*   'Soy in 1000 Gardens' is a citizen science project set up as part of the VIB Grand Challenges Programme, bringing together translational research projects with a focus on collaboration between researchers in VIB and beyond, with the potential of delivering a direct benefit to society in the immediate future.

The story goes that before she married,
one of the family's grandmothers went
to live in the palace where she learned
many recipes. One of these was *eoyukjang*
(*eo* means 'fish' and *yuk* means 'meat').
Eoyukjang is, just like chilli paste with
dried beef, a special dish that you don't
see frequently in the countryside and that
has been handed down in our family through
the generations.
When she was young, my mother loved making
eoyukjang so she would not forget its
special taste. Sadly, this did not happen
often, since quality ingredients, such as
abalone, beef, mullet, and mussels, were
costly and scarce.

– Yun Wang Soon

JANG WITH FISH AND MEAT*
EOYUKJANG

어
육
장

INGREDIENTS

600g beef brisket
1.8kg chicken
1.2kg pheasant
700g mullet (or sea
bream)
300g abalone
50g mussels
50g small shrimps
60g spring onion
210g tofu
5.5kg fermented soybeans
(meju, see p. 23)
15 litres of water
4kg salt

PREPARATION

Remove the tendons from the beef and let the
moisture from the meat evaporate by drying it in
the sun. Remove the intestines from the chicken
and pheasant and blanch the meat briefly. Rinse
the mullet and remove the head and scales. Let
everything dry in the sun for the moisture to
evaporate. Wash and clean the abalone and mussels.
Rinse the shrimps, spring onion, and tofu. Place
the beef at the bottom of the earthen jug along
with the mullet, chicken, and pheasant – in that
order. Then add the meju. Bring the water to the
boil, let it cool, and dissolve the salt. Now
continue as with a *jang* preparation. Dig a hole in
the earth and bury the jug. Fill the space between
the jug and earth with straw, seal the opening
of the jug with oiled paper and a lid. One year
later, this dish is ready to use. Take it out of
the ground and filter the *eoyukjang* to prepare
your meal.

*   RECIPE BY YUN WANG SOON.

찹쌀된장

SOYBEAN PASTE WITH GLUTINOUS RICE*
CHAPSSALDOENJANG

INGREDIENTS

5.5kg fermented soybeans
(meju see p. 23)
4kg salt
15 litres of water
1kg glutinous rice
(chapssal see p. 27)
500g chilli powder

PREPARATION

Add salt to the meju and dissolve in chilled water to soak the *jang*. Let this ferment for 50 to 70 days. Then separate the *jang* into meju and soy sauce. Soak the glutinous rice in water for more than 6 hours and steam until done. Add the steamed glutinous rice and chilli powder to the meju, stir to obtain a homogeneous mixture, and let it ferment for at least 6 months.

If you want your *jang* to be more balanced, you must add cereals. Glutinous rice is the grain of preference, but barley rice will also do. If you do not have that, you could add wheat flour for a good *jang*. I follow my mother's advice and always take glutinous rice to mix into my *jang*.

– Yun Wang Soon

* RECIPE BY YUN WANG SOON.

My mother used to say, "The best chilli paste is chilli paste with dried beef, then chilli paste with glutinous rice, and then chilli paste with barley." When spring came, she climbed a high mountain behind our village and went foraging for all sorts of wild vegetables, such as eagle fern and chrysanthemums, which she then cooked right away. She added chilli paste and soybean paste to make wild, plant-based bibimbap*. In summer, she plucked the young leaves from lettuces she had previously planted in the front garden and added chilli paste to prepare a delicious geotjeori**. Put some rice in the middle of the leaf, press it together and eat it in one big mouthful. A truly unforgettable taste.

– Yun Wang Soon

GOOD TO KNOW

*   Bibimbap is a well-known Korean rice dish, originally meaning 'mixed rice'. The idea is to mix the rice bowl with the topping and sauce (*jang*-based) until all the flavours have beautifully blended. The region, the season, and the maker offer endless variations on this dish.

** Geotjeori is a kind of instant kimchi salad that you serve immediately, without letting it ferment.

찹
쌀
고
추
장

CHILLI PASTE WITH GLUTINOUS RICE*
CHAPSSALGOCHUJANG

INGREDIENTS

800g glutinous rice
(chapssal, see p. 27)
900g malt flour**
1.2kg chilli powder
600g fermented soybean
powder (meju, see p. 23)
660g coarse salt
11 litres of water

PREPARATION

Rinse the glutinous rice, soak in water for 12
hours, drain and grind to a fine mash.
Dissolve the malt flour in lukewarm water (about
40 °C) and let it soak for more than half an
hour so that the enzymes can develop. Wait for
the sediment to settle and keep only the clear
liquid. Now mix the glutinous rice with the clear
malt water and stir well to avoid lumps. This is
glutinous rice water.
Boil the glutinous rice water for 3 hours at 60
to 70 °C so that the sugars can release. Let
this simmer until a third of the original volume
remains and the water has turned brown.
Leave the glutinous rice water to cool for a
few minutes and then add the meju. Mix until
homogeneous, then add the chilli powder. Mix until
everything is fully dissolved. Season with salt
and put the resulting mix in a jug. Sprinkle with
salt and put in a spot with plenty of sunlight.

GOOD TO KNOW

*   RECIPE BY YUN WANG SOON.

**   Malt and malt flour are usually made from barley that is germinated and
       dried, activating enzymes in the seeds that convert starch into maltose
       (malt sugar).

CORDYCEPS SOY SAUCE*
DONGCHUNGHACHOGANJANG

INGREDIENTS

4kg salt
15 litres of water
5.5kg fermented soybeans
(*meju*, see p. 23)
200g cordyceps*

PREPARATION

Add the salt to the water and dissolve it to make brine water. Let this infuse for 5 to 7 days. Rinse and prepare the *jangdok* (see p. 27). Put the appropriate amount of *meju* in the pot and then carefully pour in the salty water excluding the settled residues.

On a sunny day, open the lid of the jar and cover it again before the sun goes down. Repeat this for 50 to 70 days and then divide the *jang* into meju and soy sauce. Next, add the cordyceps to the soy sauce and cook at high heat. Skim off the foam that has formed. Turn down the heat and simmer for 30 minutes. Put the still warm soy sauce in a jar and close with a lid. Store the pot in a sunny spot.

GOOD TO KNOW

*　　RECIPE BY YUN WANG SOON.

**　　Cordyceps is a mould that grows into a fungus. It is used in traditional Korean cuisine for its medicinal and culinary qualities.

When I was young, we kept countless silkworms at the house. They lived off our home-grown mulberry leaves. If we were short of leaves to feed them, my mother would go foraging. When the silkworms were grown, we sold their cocoons. First, we picked the silk threads from the cocoons and hung these on a loom to weave clothes. Once all the silk was extracted, mother took out the pupa and gave us this very nutritious food. Whatever was left, mother let it decompose until fungi developed (cordyceps). Once those cordyceps were ready for use, she stuffed a chicken with them and cooked it. Or she incorporated them into some other dish. Really remarkable was when she mixed the cordyceps into her soy sauce, which gave it a truly unique taste.

– Yun Wang Soon

SHIITAKE SOY SAUCE*
PYOGOGANJANG

표
고
간
장

INGREDIENTS

500g dried shiitakes
5.5kg *meju* (see p. 23)
4kg salt
15 litres of water

PREPARATION

Dissolve the salt in the water to make the brine. Let it rest for 5 to 7 days. Rinse the *jangdok* (jar) well before use. Add the right amount of *meju* and carefully pour in the brine water without the sediment. On a sunny day, open the lid of the jar and close it again before the sun sets. Repeat this for 50 to 70 days and then divide the *jang* into *meju* and soy sauce. Add shiitakes to the soy sauce and cook at high heat. Remove the scum that has formed with a skimmer and let it simmer for half an hour at low temperature. Pour the still hot soy sauce into a jar and close the lid. Store it in a spot with lots of sunlight.

*　　RECIPE BY YUN WANG SOON.

On rainy days, rather than working in the fields, mother stayed home and kept herself busy knitting or sewing. As soon as the rain stopped, she slipped on her coat, put on her boots and marched to the other side of the mountain, walking stick in hand.

I can still see her there, up in those mountains, wet from the rain, water droplets falling from the leaves. With a cheeky smile on her face, she turns round and shouts: "Look, the wild mushrooms that grow at night, enokis, chestnut mushrooms, shiitakes, oyster mushrooms... They appear everywhere!"

She was an expert in distinguishing the poisonous mushrooms from the edible ones. For her soy sauce, she used dried shiitakes and dried pollock heads, with a bunch of other ingredients.

– Yun Wang Soon

Saying that Gu Bon Il is passionate about *jang* would be an understatement. She emits tremendous energy and sleeps only three hours a night. Otherwise, she would not have enough time to do all that is needed for all the *jang* she produces. She strives to spread the tradition and knowledge of *jang* culture with a specific focus on the *jang* makers to come. For them especially, she has developed highly simplified and less time-consuming *jang* making methods. Her greatest wish is that her recipes will stand the test of time and will be handed down to future generations.

Gu Bon Il has over twenty years of experience under her belt making *jang*, but it was only five years ago that she started a company with her husband to produce and sell fermented seasonings. Currently, the couple export to Hong Kong, send samples to the US, and dream of selling their *jang* in Europe. The soy sauce they distribute is at least three years old and has won awards in 2019, 2020, and 2021.

Gu Bon Il is 67 years old and her husband Lee Seon Geun is 70.

FIST-THICK FERMENTED SOYBEANS*
JUMEOKMEJU

INGREDIENTS

dried soybeans
appropriate amount of
water

PREPARATION

Rinse the soybeans three or four times with water
and put them in a pressure cooker. Add water to
about the length of one finger from the bottom
of the pot. When the boiling signal sounds, wait
about 3 minutes before turning off the heat. Wait
for all the steam to escape. When everything has
cooled down, place the pressure cooker back on the
heat. Shake the pan so that the beans on top fall
down and the bottom beans come up. At the next
boiling signal, wait another 3 or 4 minutes and
turn off the heat. Place the pan on the heat again
until the boiling signal sounds, then turn off the
heat once again. Once all the steam is released,
pour the beans into a sieve. They are well
cooked if you can crush them between thumb and
forefinger. Puree the beans with a large mortar
while they are still hot. Shape the pureed paste
into fist-thick blocks. Place these *meju* blocks in
a colander to dry for three to four days. Turn the
meju over regularly, as moisture can cause rot if
any side does not properly dry. After this, when
the surface of the *meju* has sufficiently dried,
place the *meju* in a clean cardboard box and let
it ferment for five days. Turn the *meju* over once
a day. White and yellow fungi will develop. Five
days later, place the meju in a colander, where
it can continue to dry in a cool and dark place.
After ten to fifteen days, you can make *jang* from
this *meju*.

GOOD TO KNOW

If too much mould has formed on the surface, brush it off, rinse briefly
with water, and then make your *jang*.

*   RECIPE BY GU BON IL.

주먹메주

FERMENTED SOYBEAN PASTE*
DOENJANG

된
장

INGREDIENTS

4kg *jumeokmeju*
(see p. 190)
10 litres of water
1.25g salt

PREPARATION

Grind the prepared *meju* with a mortar to make *jang*. Add the water and salt. Mix into a smooth puree, put in an earthen jug, and press firmly. Cover the top with a cotton cloth and put a lid on it. If you make small portions, take a suitable container and cover it with a kitchen towel. Put it in a place in your kitchen where it is clearly visible. After seven days, the paste is ready to ripen in your fridge for a month or two. When the fermentation is finished, the paste can be served.

GOOD TO KNOW

You may flavour the water by boiling it with salt, dried yellow pollack, and some dried shiitakes. Cooled, you can use this clear broth as a substitute for water; it will make your soybean paste even tastier.

*   RECIPE BY GU BON IL.

청
국
장

FAST FERMENTED SOYBEAN PASTE*
CHEONGGUKJANG

INGREDIENTS

dried soybeans
water

PREPARATION

One day in advance, soak the beans in ample water
for 8 hours. Rinse the beans three times with
water and steam for half an hour. Let them rest
for 10 to 20 minutes. When the preparation reaches
a temperature of 35 °C, wrap the beans in a cotton
cloth. Put in a high place in the kitchen where it
can ferment for about 30 hours. Your *cheonggukjang*
has worked well when a whitish layer has formed
on the beans and mucus is visible when you stir
through the mass. Well-fermented *cheonggukjang*
should smell like a strong cheese. You must use
it within 24 hours, the rest can be stored in the
freezer.

GOOD TO KNOW

Soybeans should be sufficiently cooked for the proteins to break down more
easily. You can consider them cooked when they go red and are easily crushed
between thumb and forefinger.
Steaming is preferred over boiling as this would control the moisture and
mould later on. Steaming lessens the strong smell as well.

*   RECIPE BY GU BON IL.

FERMENTED SOY SAUCE*
GANJANG

간
장

INGREDIENTS

2.5 litres of water
500g salt
1kg *jumeokmeju*
(see recipe p. 190)
handful of kelp
2 dried shiitakes
2 Korean dates (*daechu*)
1 stick of activated
charcoal (optional)**

PREPARATION

Dissolve the salt in the water and put this salt
water in a sterilized or well-cleaned earthen
jug. Put the dried *jumeokmeju* in and add the kelp,
shiitake and dates for adding aroma. Charcoal
is a purifying agent and is said to prevent poor
mould formation. Make sure that the *meju* remains
submerged, you can perhaps put a heavy object on
top. Close tightly with a cotton cloth and leave
to ferment for at least 2 months. Next, remove the
jumeokmeju, coarsely puree it to obtain *doenjang*,
and store in the refrigerator. You can let the
moisture continue to mature into *ganjang*.

GOOD TO KNOW

*   RECIPE BY GU BON IL.

**   Activated charcoal is different from the fireplace or barbecue variety,
        which is not suitable for consumption. Activated charcoal requires a
        special treatment. Hence, it is best to buy it (for instance, I find
        mine online).

The ratio is 1 kilogram *meju* to 2.5 litres of water to 500 grams of salt, so
4 kilogram (of *meju)* to 10 litres of water to 2 kilograms of salt.

GU BON IL'S FERMENTED SOYBEAN PASTE WITH SOY SAUCE*
GU BON IL GANJANGDOENJANG

구
본
일
의
간
장
된
장

INGREDIENTS

500ml water, bottled or
boiled and cooled
300ml soy sauce (any
type)
400g fermented soybean
powder (*meju*, see p. 23)
20 to 30g chilli powder
(optional)
100ml extra soy sauce
(optional)

PREPARATION

Mix the water with the soy sauce. Since the soy
sauce has already been fermented, use this instead
of salt. Add the fermented soybean powder and let
it rest for about 10 minutes. Add chilli powder
to taste. If you do, mix in extra soy sauce to
retain the smooth texture. Put the freshly made
soybean paste in a sterilized or well-cleaned jar
(glass, plastic, anything suitable for storing
food). Gently press the paste to remove the air
and prevent unwanted mould from forming. Finally,
just before closing the jar, pour a small dash
of soy sauce on top of the soybean paste. Leave
the *doenjang* for a month in the refrigerator to
ferment. This soybean paste has a maximum shelf
life of one year.

*   RECIPE BY GU BON IL.

Chung Chung Kee is cultural translator and traditional food researcher affiliated with the Centre for Education and Research into Nutrition and Body in Paju, Gyeonggi-do. He is researching and translating the *Imwon Geyongjeji*, the mid-19th-century Korean encyclopaedia that describes in detail all aspects of life in rural areas. *Imwon* means 'a rural area' and *Gyeongjeji* means 'a domestic life'.

This encyclopaedia provides in-depth knowledge and guidance on sixteen different topics considered essential to living in the countryside. Themes range from rural life, agriculture, food supplies in case of scarcity, astronomy and the Confucian aristocracy, to architecture, music, and family rituals.

The eighth book, entitled *Jeongjoji*, covers 'food and breweries' with scientific accounts of recipes for dishes, drinks, and sauces from the era of the late Joseon Dynasty (1392-1897). The book offers an introduction to various Korean recipes, with special attention to wholesome meals based on medical knowledge. It gives information on seasonings, spices, and 160 methods for preparing traditional wines.

The author of *Imwon Gyeongjeji* (113 volumes, 52 books, published in 1827) was Seo Yu Gu (1764-1845), a prominent scholar of the Korean Confucian school.

Chung Chung Kee's research is particularly concerned with the preparation of fermented sauces, such as *jang* and *sikcho* (vinegar), and fermented alcoholic beverages, such as *buuiju*. Also known as *dongdongju*, *buuiju* refers to the particles that float on the surface like ants on a mush when fermentation has reached an advanced stage.

For some years, Chung Chung Kee has been guiding several enthusiasts who study together and reproduce some of the original *Jeongjoji* recipes on a monthly basis.

On one of my trips to Korea, I received an invitation from their study group. They welcomed me into their workroom where, to my surprise, I was treated to an abundant, festive meal. The dishes and drinks were delicious and were all prepared according to the recipes they had studied – a stark contrast with today's commercial Korean flavours. This surprise feast remains one of my most memorable meals in Korea.

Namchojang refers to what we know today as *gochujang* (red chilli paste). Since *namchojang* appeared early in the history of *gochujang* and contains only a small amount of chilli powder, it would no longer be recognized as red chilli paste today. The method of mixing fermented soybean powder with glutinous rice flour, chilli powder, and soy sauce to make *namchojang* further developed into modern *gochujang* preparations. This went hand-in-hand with a radical increase in the amount of red chilli powder, an evolution resulting from economic prosperity and a change in people's taste preferences.

– Chung Chung Kee

남
초
장

FERMENTED CHILLI PASTE*
NAMCHOJANG

INGREDIENTS

an appropriate amount of
soy sauce (*sonmat*, see
p. 20)
500g fermented soybean
powder (*meju*, see p. 23)
15g chilli powder
50g glutinous rice flour
(*chapssal*, see p. 27)

PREPARATION

Add the soy sauce to the fermented soybean powder,
the chilli powder, and the glutinous rice flour
and mix well until it is sufficiently thickened.
Put the chilli paste in a small jug and leave this
to dry in the sun.

ORIGINAL RECIPE (*Imwon Geyongjeji, Jeongjoji, Miryojiryujang***)

Remove sand and stones from the soybeans and prepare the *meju* (fermented
soybeans) as usual. For every 10 *seung****, use 0.3 *seung* chilli powder and
1 *seung* glutinous rice flour. Add a large dash of high-quality soy sauce to
the three ingredients and stir well to thicken the mixture. Put the mixture
in a small jug and let it dry in the sun.
It is also possible to add 0.5 *seung* of toasted sesame powder, but this will
make the sauce greasy and dry, and cause it to spoil faster. If you add too
much glutinous rice, the taste will become unpleasantly sour. And best be
careful with the chilli powder, or it will be too spicy.

GOOD TO KNOW

*   RECIPE BY CHUNG CHUNG KEE.

**   *Miryojiryu* can refer to salt, *jang*, tofu, vinegar, oil, malt, yeast, and
        sauce.
***   1 *seung* = 2 litres.

두
부
남
초
장

FERMENTED CHILLI PASTE WITH TOFU*
TOFOE NAMCHOJANG

INGREDIENTS

1 packet of tofu
15g chilli powder
250g fermented soybean
powder (*meju*, see p. 23)
50g glutinous rice flour
(*chapssal*, see p. 27)
an appropriate amount of
soy sauce (*sonmat*, see
p. 20)

PREPARATION

Put the tofu in a cotton cloth and gently squeeze
out the moisture. Make sure to remove as much
moisture as possible – do this with whatever
you have available. Mix the tofu, chilli powder,
fermented soybean powder, and glutinous rice
flour. Add the soy sauce and mix well.
Put the prepared chilli paste in a small jug and
put in the sun to dry.

ORIGINAL RECIPE (*Imwon Geyongjeji, Jeongjoji, Miryojiryujang*)

Make the tofu with 10 *seung* of soybeans and squeeze gently to remove
the moisture from the tofu. Mix the red chilli powder with the other
ingredients, put in a jug, and dry in the sun.

* RECIPE BY CHUNG CHUNG KEE.

Jukjangyeong is a company specialising in traditionally produced soybean paste. The company name, *Jukjangyeong*, stems from the village name, *Jukjangmyeon*, and *jayeon*, the Korean word for 'nature'. The founders have a special link with the village thanks to its sisterly relationship of 'one company, one village,' a pact strongly committed to a win-win narrative between companies and the countryside. When you walk onto the property, you see fermentation pots arrayed as far as the eye can see. There are several *jangdokdae* (see p. 27), with about 3000 *jangdok* (see p. 27), filled with *jang* from various vintages.

Wine and *jang* have similar characteristics. The basic ingredients (beans and grapes) are different, but both become what they are through the processes of fermentation and maturation. Just like the same wine tastes different depending on the year, the taste of *jang* will vary according to the period in which it was produced. A 2011 soybean paste has a deep and lingering flavour, while a 2014 paste is renowned for its balance.

The natural environment has a considerable impact on both products. Jukjangyeon is situated in the valley of the Taebaek Mountains, over one hour from Pohang, Gyeongsangbuk-do, in the southeast of the peninsula. This region benefits from sun and wind all day long and all year round. The air is clean and not yet polluted, with a significant temperature difference between winter and summer.

– Jeong Yeon Tae, CEO van Jukjangyeon

Only three ingredients are needed to produce traditional *jang*: soybeans, salt, and water. Therefore, the quality of these constituents is crucial to make a truly tasty *jang*.

The soybeans we use are grown locally near Pohang and Cheongsong. The sun-dried Sinan salt is left to mature for a long time before use. The purified spring water comes from 200 metres beneath the surface of Jukjangyeon and thus contains many minerals. Every year, at the start of a new season, twenty mothers from the village are busy produce a huge amount of soybean paste.

– Jeong Yeon Tae, CEO van Jukjangyeon

ACKNOWLEDGMENTS

- **Frederik Sioen** for your love, support, and enthusiasm.
- **Go Young Joo** for your friendship, hospitality, warmth, and wisdom.
- **Kim Zin Ho & Jang Bo Hyun, Mathieu Cieters & Lore Snauwaert** for the elegant aesthetics.
- **Selma Franssen, Doortje Callaert, Alan Anderson and Nikki Legon** for elevating my words to a higher level.
- **Yun Yeongseop** for building bridges between languages.
- **Yun Wang Soon & Kim Jin Ha, Moon Sung Hee, Kim Sol & Byeon Jong Hyun, Chung Chung Kee, Yu Mi Young & Kim Ji Hyun, Kim Eun Young, Kim Do Yun, Jeong Yeon Tae, Wook Wan Seunim,** for your hospitality, enthusiasm, and inspiration.
- **Caroline Kesteleyn** for the beautiful ceramics.
- **Julian Quintart,** for the connections.

WITH THE SUPPORT OF

- **Het Vlaams Instituut voor Biotechnologie** , with special thanks to **Sofie Bekaert** for facilitating this collaboration.
- **De Vroente,** which combines the experience and youthful energy of three farms: **De Kollebloem, Ourobouros, and De Zonnekouter.** Together, they cultivate biodynamic quality vegetables and fruit. With character, fresh, and straight from the field. Thank you for the vegetables.

먹자! MOKJA! LET'S EAT!

Inspired by the Korean food philosophy, Mokja presents simple and pure recipes with a wide variety of tastes, colours, and textures. Through catering, workshops and pop-ups, Ae Jin Huys brings people into contact with the quintessence of Korean cuisine. She also trains professionals and is an author at publishing house Lannoo.
www.mokja.be

TEXT AND RECIPES: Ae Jin Huys
COPYWRITING: Selma Franssen
TRANSLATION TO ENGLISH: Doortje Callaert
PHOTOGRAPHY: sustain-works, with the exception of pp. 204-207; photos provided by Jukjangyeon
FOODSTYLING: Jang Bo Hyun
GRAPICH DESIGN: StudioStudio.be ☺☺

www.lannoo.com
Please register on our website to receive a newsletter with updates on recent books and interesting, exclusive offers. .

If you have observations or questions, please contact our editorial office:
redactielifestyle@lannoo.com

© Ae Jin Huys & Uitgeverij Lannoo nv, Tielt, 2023
D/2023/45/133 — NUR 440
ISBN: 978 94 014 8934 8

Notification requested by 'jang master' Yun Wang Soon: all recipes from her hand are shared exclusively with the author (Ae Jin Huys) and copying or sharing by third parties for commercial purposes is prohibited.